ROMANCE YOUR PLAN

TAKING GENRE FICTION MARKETING TO THE NEXT LEVEL

ZOE YORK

ZoYo Press

London, Ontario, CANADA

www.ZoeYork.com

www.romanceyourbrand.com

In memory of my beloved Dziadzio, whose life didn't turn out exactly the way he planned but was pretty freaking epic nonetheless

Beat them at their own game
(but do it with integrity)

ABOUT THIS BOOK

After writing a genre fiction series, what's next? Writing another one, that will both please existing fans and find you new readers at the same time. Zoe York has been there a dozen times. In this follow up to *Romance Your Brand*, the *USA Today* bestselling author breaks down how to pick the right marketing plan for your brand, your books, and your readers.

Let's talk about:

- scheduling sales
- planning releases
- brand re-vamping
- audience growth
- fandom building
- goal setting
- weathering low points
- kicking off a new series

ABOUT THE AUTHOR

Photo: Regina Wamba

Zoe York is a thirteen-time USA Today bestselling author of contemporary romance, often with military heroes, and always with scorching heat between the pages. Between her two pen names (she also writes erotic romance as Ainsley Booth), she has published more than fifty books since her debut in 2013 with *What Once Was Perfect*. Notable hits include *Prime Minister* (*USA Today* bestseller twice, in 2016 and 2017), the *SEALs of Summer* anthologies (*New York Times* bestsellers in 2014 and 2015), and twenty books in the fan-favourite Canadian small town series, Pine Harbour and Wardham. She is a mouthy and proud member of Toronto Romance Writers.

The title of this book really says it all. My goal here is to help you romance *your* plan, a little or a lot. This is not a step-by-step How to Market A Genre Fiction Book plan, because I don't think such a thing really exists beyond the following:

- Write a Book
- Package the Book
- Launch the Book
- Maintain Book Visibility Over Time (Periodically or Steadily)
- Write Another Similar Book, and then Another

The better you hit each of those points, the more success you'll have. That's *the* plan.

Your plan is going to be some variation on that, and it is *your* plan that needs to be romanced. I am the first person to talk about which of the Generally Good Ideas I struggle with (another similar book? But I want to write all the things! And can't they launch themselves?), so please know that this book is coming from a place of *I get it.*

But I think, if you picked up this book, it's because you also want to advance your career and maybe make more money.

And in that pursuit (moving the needle for yourself), everything I talk about is going to be something you need to measure against where you were, and where you want to go.

As you read this book, always ask yourself—does this advice apply to *my* plan? If not, it's still interesting information to consider. *Oh, that's how someone else might do it.* And file the suggestion away.

If it is meant to be part of your plan, it will come back to you at the right time.

Harder to absorb will be the beats that you definitely recognize as applying to your plan, but you have some essential pain around actually *doing* it. *Yes this part applies to me...and I don't like it.*

"I don't want to do this thing that I really know will work," is a thought I have regularly. I'm not sure we talk enough in the book world about how authors are artists and artists are mercurial creatures with complicated mental health stuff. We are! And we often suffer from anxiety and depression at a higher rate than the rest of the world.

I don't want to pretend I have the best plan ever. I really don't. And the last thing I want this book to do is make anyone feel like book marketing is harder than they thought.

So please, be extraordinarily gentle on yourself. Nobody has their shit entirely together, nobody, and the more we talk about how we're all just doing the best we can with what we have, the better we'll all be.

You might also hit some ouchy points where you think, *I can't afford that.*

I have been there. I have. When I started writing, my husband was going through a very deep, dark PTSD-fuelled depression, and it affected every part of our lives, including our income. I couldn't afford a BookBub featured deal until I was in a multi-author boxed set that did well enough to pay for that BookBub deal.

Barter what you need to. Put off the CPC ads—there, I'll say that up front in the foreword. Paying for ads out of pocket is a luxury, it's optional, and most of this book is about romancing your plan without them.

Do everything else, and your business will start to generate more money. A business that generates more money can, in time, be a business that invests in things like Facebook ads.

Until then, you're going to focus on being a business that is singularly focused on promoting your brand through word of mouth on social media and zero-barrier-to-entry loss leaders.

And to do that, you're going to figure out (with my help) what needs to go, what definitely should stay, and which parts of your plan need to get sharper.

It occurs to me as I read this back that I'm making a lot of assumptions about who is reading this. I think you're already published, and probably familiar with or already experienced with the indie side of genre fiction publishing. If you are not, if you grabbed this book for some other reason, I recommend pausing here and going to my YouTube videos, my blog, and my first book before continuing.

On that bossy note, let's get into it. We have books to promote!

This book is divided into three sections. The first section is the think-y part, where I lay out my philosophy about publishing and how book marketing works from my indie author perspective. Each of the five chapters in Part I has homework at the end of it, building on the chapter before it.

Part II is a reference section, breaking down individual marketing actions. Less homework, more bullet point lists. I do love a good list.

And Part III is where we get to the actual Plan Stuff, but please don't skip right there unless you're a read-out-of-order type of person, because the context around the marketing steps is really what makes an effective, move-the-needle kind of plan.

PART ONE

CONTEXT FIRST, PLANNING SECOND

CHAPTER ONE

A BIRD'S EYE VIEW OF BOOK MARKETING

WHEN I STARTED PUBLISHING BOOKS, I thought book marketing was:

- getting a blog tour
- distributing advance review copies of books
- sharing teasers from the book on social media
- eventually getting into paid advertising (I didn't want to do this for my first book)
- knowing I would make my first-in-series free once I had four books in the series
- having an email newsletter from day one
- having a Facebook reader group from day one

That's a pretty decent seven-point plan, to be honest.

All of that was based on advice from others and observing what successful authors seemed to do. (The last point is indie publishing specific, but if you replace it with a 99 cent loss leader promotion, it's still a pretty universal list of Good Marketing Ideas.)

But that action list is not what book marketing really is. It's the end result of a marketing plan that really works best on a frontlist release launched with momentum. We're going to go all the way back to the start, to a bird's eye view of marketing, to make sure that the end result is mapped to our goals and where we are at in the publishing marketplace.

In my first nonfiction book, *Romance Your Brand*, I wanted my takeaway message for writers to be, "your brand will improve if you tighten the focus of what you write."

In *this* book I hope one of the takeaway messages is, "your business plan will improve if you tighten the focus on what you are marketing, and to whom you are marketing that product."

Really rolls off the tongue. Let's condense it down. **"Your plan is both: what you are marketing and who you are marketing it to."**

Once you have those two elements tight and focused, then the *how* to market gets infinitely easier.

Who you are marketing to is your audience.
What you are marketing is your product.

That latter point—<u>what</u> you are marketing—is the entire focus of *Romance Your Brand*. So if you haven't read that I recommend going back, starting there, and making sure the product that you are currently trying to promote is in fact the right product for your brand. A gut-level check is to ask yourself, how excited are you to promote this product?

Author enthusiasm is the single most important factor in building a successful business. If we don't both believe in our product and think everyone should read it…how are we ever going to sustain a lasting marketing plan?

(And I know I keep saying product instead of book. That's deliberate, because the focus of this book is marketing, and in order to think about that clearly, it's better to think of your books as products and not the uniquely perfect artistic creations that we both know they are. Once you set them out onto the commercial market, that is not *all* they are, at least.)

But after author enthusiasm, the second most important factor in building a successful business is learning how to objectively assess your books. How to know when they're hitting market expectations, and how to know when they're missing (and why).

One tool to help in that analysis is what I call A Bird's Eye View of Book Marketing.

A Bird's Eye View of Book Marketing

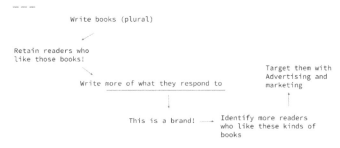

Once we understand the pathway from writing books to promoting them (including an objective assessment of which products to promote, and to whom), then the terms warm and cold audiences make a heck of a lot more sense.

A warm audience is made up of the readers you retain after they have enjoyed one of your books; a cold or lukewarm audience are readers you target for reasons, who might like your books because they like similar books. More on this shortly.

A Bird's Eye View of Book Marketing

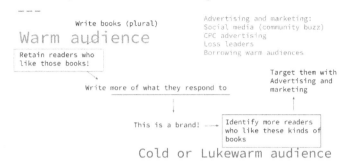

Three key takeaways from this view:

- Marketing begins with market research
- Brand only exists in the marketplace
- Advertising works when you know who you are targeting and why

Your job as your internal Marketing Director is to understand this market analysis; get that right, and tasks can be outsourced (to yourself or to others). More on this later!

So as we move into the nitty-gritty of book marketing, let's remember that every individual promotion effort sits in this larger connected web of actions. In the next chapter, I'm going to start with the absolute basics. It will be the first of many checklists in this book, and I will again encourage you to be soft with the items on that list. Some will be for you to implement immediately, others will take time—either to figure out the resources needed, or to wrap your head around the *why* of the item.

When you have concerns, come back to this chapter. Look at the Bird's Eye View of Marketing schematic and think, where does this fit?

Homework: On a blank piece of paper, draw out your own bird's eye view of marketing. (Feel free to copy my diagram exactly) This will be the template upon which you build your marketing plan.

CHAPTER TWO

MARKETING BASICS

IT WOULD AMAZING if we could write books and people just magically found them, but that's not how it works. Finding and growing a reader base is hard, steady, and sometimes slow work. In this chapter, I'm going to cover the basics of what every single author can do in order to have a foundation that will retain readers they find.

This list includes:

- email mailing list
- website
- social media
- reader groups
- ebook formatting with a mind for marketing

These elements make up the foundation for capturing readers who enjoy your work. That is the single best advantage an author can have in the digital book product sphere: reader retention.

And right off the bat, some of these foundational elements may have you bristling—as I said in the foreword, that's okay. Be soft with these suggestions, take what is useful, and set the rest aside for a while.

But I would encourage you, as I do myself on a regular basis, to think about why we don't want to try something that works for others. Is it because we don't like it as a consumer? Is it because we wish we didn't have to do this for ourselves? Is it because it doesn't align with our taste, our aesthetic, or our principles?

The last one is an excellent reason to skip something. The rest…maybe a reason to consider outsourcing that part of the foundation creation or maintenance. I have a chapter, "Outsource It!" later in the book to address the big "I. Don't. Wanna." elements in a business plan.

But right now, let's go over all the elements most authors should[1] have in their business plan. Some of these will be expanded on later in the book as well. Email mailing lists as a to-do list item is fundamentally different from the ways we can maximize email marketing as authors, for example. But let's make sure we can walk before we run.

EMAIL MAILING LISTS

An email marketing list, aka an author newsletter, is a database of direct contact information from every reader who has liked your books and wants to know more about your work. This is gold! I really feel confident saying everyone should have a mailing list. You want it to be managed by a third party that specializes in this sort of thing. There are a number of email marketing services that offer free accounts until you reach X number of subscribers. Don't worry about how much they cost once you pass that threshold—at that point, you can make the mailing list pay for itself. You want to have a sign-up form embedded on your website, and a link to a sign-up landing page in your ebooks. Then, when you have a new release, you send those people an email. That is the warm audience marketing loop in a nutshell, and without an email newsletter, it's so much harder to do. Put this at the top of your to-do list.

WEBSITES

You need one. It doesn't need to be fancy. There are free options as well. Your own dedicated website is passive marketing, and for a long time it won't do much, but eventually people will Google your name or your series and the more interesting your website is, with bonus content about the series or at the very least a **reading order**, the more useful it will be to your readers. **A blog** is another option, *if you are so inclined*, where you could retain interested readers. This is one example where there are outliers who don't have one and still have success, and I'll just say this: hoping to be an outlier is not a business plan.

SOCIAL MEDIA

Like a blog, almost everything under this category should be considered *if you are so inclined*. But a lot of networking and reader engagement happens on social media, so you still want to grab this real estate even if you don't use it right now—that might change in the future, and then you'll have the branded platform to use. As I said at the top, if your principles prevent you from using a specific site, I'm not going to tell you that you're wrong on that point. You may need to lean harder on another element of your marketing plan, and your reach may be different. For me, I grab @zoeyorkwrites as the username on every major social media platform.

READER GROUPS

They used to be on Yahoo. Some authors have forums on their own sites. Then Facebook took over and most people pivoted there. Today, people are gathering readers on Patreon and Discord, too. *Tomorrow it could be something else, which is why a mailing list is a good backup here—so you can flex as the market shifts.* For me, I'm still on Facebook, and my reader group is a way to tap into the social media-savvy readership in my genre. Some authors like to do a shared group, and share the admin burden. That's a good option for the reluctant about social media writer. Worth underlining that a reader group, while often hosted on social media, is different from staking claim to your public-facing options as a brand on those same platforms.

EBOOK FORMATTING WITH A MIND FOR MARKETING

This is the most important thing that I want you to take away from this introduction, and it's the only time I'm going to say anything critical about selling a book to a publisher: if you control your ebook formatting, you have better access to your readers. You can give readers specific CTAs (calls to action) with regard to signing up for your mailing list, reader group, visiting your website, and clicking through to the next book in the series.

Most publishers don't think any of this matters. They are dead wrong, and that's why they're losing the digital marketplace to indie authors.

Some publishers are smart, and they're doing all of this...for themselves. And a few publishers are even smarter, and they're including their authors' mailing list links in the bios, because they know that a happy author is one who will stay with them. If you are thinking of traditionally publishing a series you designed, make sure this is a question that comes up in the negotiations.

As a reader, I see authors start over again at square one with new series all the time; if you have a strong mailing list of people that liked series A, you can tell them about series B, and start off in a much stronger place. You only collect that data—people who liked your books—from links in the front and backs of those books.

You will also funnel people social media from your ebook formatting, if you include those links.

For me, when I release a new book, I see: sign-ups to my mailing list; requests to join my Facebook reader group; new follows on my Facebook and Instagram accounts. And often those are different people, without overlap. Only the superfans follow you everywhere.

By securing these foundational elements, you cover all the bases for the very different types of readers that exist in the world.

Homework: Map which of these foundational elements you already have onto your bird's eye view of marketing (they all cluster around the first arrow, retaining readers who like your books). Whichever you don't yet have go onto a to-do list. We'll come back to that!

---

1. Should is a such a loaded term. The vast majority of the time i try to edit it out of my work and my opinions. But on this chapter, the very first chapter in this book, I feel confident saying, for example, all authors should have an email marketing list. How they use it, where it's hosted, how it's delivered…that's where the variety can come in.

   Of course there are authors who don't have websites. Who have opted out of a social media site. But they're hustling extra hard somewhere else. Know what the price is! More on that in the next chapter.

CHAPTER THREE

UNDERSTANDING THE READERSCAPE

I LIKE to talk about genre fiction readers as "the reader-scape" because that term evokes images of something vast, stretching as far as you can see and then even further.

It's important to remember that the readers we know, and maybe the readers that we are, are not *all that readers are*.

For example, there are more corners of Romance-landia than any individual romance author or blogger or voracious reader could ever name. There are many we will never bump into, but in those corners, people are reading and writing a ton of content.

I know a writer who has a couple of secret pen names, in two very different sub-genres of romance, and those reader pools have almost no overlap with each other in terms of newsletter subscribers and social media followers. It's a mistake to think that the readers we can see are representative of all of our readers as a whole, but it's still telling that those two metrics are quite different for the pen names. In fact, when she shared the names—all reasonably successful—I had never noticed any of them in my own regular search for something delicious to read.

I am a voracious romance reader, and I can't see the whole scope of my own corner of genre fiction.

So we need to be very careful about making absolute statements about what works, what doesn't, and what the publishing rules are.

We also need to guard ourselves against *others* telling us those very same things, especially when their perceptions run completely counter to what we want to write. "Billionaire heroes are *over*," I've seen on Twitter, for example.

They may be over for that writer. They may be over for the people who liked and re-tweeted that statement.

They are not over in any way for the *thousands* of people who bought that kind of romance across many, many titles yesterday.

But a tender-hearted author on Twitter, who has a

wildly sexy idea for a billionaire romance, might see that tweet and think…maybe I should shelve that idea.

Oh, no.

Please don't.

And I say that as someone who really thinks that in real life, billionaires should be taxed out of being billionaires; bring back that 70% marginal tax rate and change the world. But fiction is where we get to play with problematic content, where we can morph bad guys into good guys, and build what-if potentials. Sometimes we get it right, sometimes we miss the mark—and so we try again. But if we don't write the ideas we love the most, we will miss the mark entirely every single time.

Wealth is, as Jennifer Lynn Barnes says, a universal pleasure point, like beauty, and apple orchards[1]. There are others who dig into this so much better than I could (I like Shelf Love Podcast, for example), but on most of the things we hold ourselves back from writing—billionaires, violet eyes, families with eight handsome brothers, scrappy teenage girls who save the world, and on and on—are pleasure points people actually want more of (the violet eyes is a direct example Barnes gives in her Writing for Your Id workshop).

If you are no longer comfortable with dabbling in

the billionaire romance field, that's a different thing. Your plan can pivot you in a new direction!

But if you have a story that excites you, know that there is a healthy part of the readerscape that wants *that story*, exactly as you want to tell it, and there will be other parts that want to criticize it, and all of that is fine and normal.

[We need to normalize building boundaries between us and the important criticism of our work, too. That part of the readerscape is not for us.]

[Please do be thoughtful and considerate around avoiding harm; don't write marginalized characters as your villains or include them only as trauma porn. That's the only caveat, and it leaves a giant field of ideas wide open.]

The takeaway I want you to have from this chapter is that if the readerscape you occupy does not like what you write, that is a toxic, messy place to be in as a creator. And you might like it for other reasons, but *when you are creating,* consider spending time in other spaces—and since this genre is vast, you may not even know where those spaces are. Ask around. You may be surprised at what you find.

It's also absolutely fine to not be in any corners of the readerscape when writing, and to outsource any part of that which might be required for book promotion.

The right formula of networking + promotion + reader interaction will be different for every author. No, scratch that. It will be different for *every author's brand.*

Because you, the person who writes books, are not exactly the same as the public face of your brand as an author. If you think right now that your public face is who you really are, stop right now and put figure out what my public author persona is on your to-do list.

And then again, neither of those two identities is quite the same as the marketing manager of Your Author Brand Inc.

How we move through social media is going to be different depending on which hat we are currently wearing. The more deliberate and aware you can be in that identity switching, the easier it will be.

"Just get off social media" is not 100% functional advice for small business owners in an industry that grew out of social media (indie genre fiction), but "use social media with careful purpose when it's your brand, and however makes you happy the rest of the time" is probably closer to something that works.

But social media is not the only part of the reader-scape you will experience. Here is a rough breakdown of how I think about the different spheres of the reader-scape that I am aware of.

The Readerscape

This is very simplified, but just from this limited sketch I hope you've expanded your mental picture of where readers might exist for your books—and ergo, places for you to venture into, as one or more of the following identities: you the writer; you the public face of your brand; or your brand's marketing manager.

The vastness of this readerscape comes into play in penultimate and final steps of the bird's eye view of marketing, identifying and targeting more readers who are like the readers you have already retained through the marketing basics in the previous chapter.

The readerscape encapsulates all the readers you can see, while still acknowledging to yourself that there are many that you can't imagine just yet. This diagram hopefully captures cold audiences, hot audiences, and everything in between, and that's what we will dig into in the next chapter.

Homework: Map out your own readerscape diagram. You can get really granular and more specific than mine. List any deal sites you subscribe to, any specific authors whose readers you might want to target, any blogs that cover what you write.

---

1. This is a nod to Dr. Barnes' work on Id Lists, a writing tool I positively fan-girl over at every turn. Apple orchards are on my id list, no, I don't think they're as universal as wealth and beauty, but I like lists of three, and I couldn't think of a third item quite as universal as wealth and beauty.

CHAPTER FOUR

AUDIENCES: COLD, WARM, HOT

HERE'S what authors should know about audiences before they tackle a marketing plan.

- Cold audiences: new to you in every way.
- Warm audiences: aware of you, possibly interested in your product.
- Hot audiences: they've already pre-ordered, but need love and attention. *see also, fandoms

When you start out, everyone is a cold audience, and getting over that hump is one of the hardest things any writer will ever do. Then you sell a few books, and your warm audience is your best friend, your Uncle Matt, and a couple of people who randomly happen to find your books in the magical way we want a LOT of people to find out books (but that usually doesn't happen). It's very normal to have a warm audience of five.

First myth to bust here: If you have a warm audience of five, if you have a newsletter of sixty people, if you put a book up for pre-order and...crickets...you're some kind of failure.

You're not. You're me, in fact! Hey, buddy, I've been there. The Uncle Matt mentioned two paragraphs up? Literally, my Uncle Matt, in my Facebook reader group. He left once the group started to grow (but his sister-in-law, my aunt Nicole, has stuck around to this day).

Second myth: Once you sell a lot of books (I've done that! More than once!), you've got a "big audience" and they buy all your books.

Ha! I wish.

One big takeaway I wish I could teach other authors is that your audience—your mailing list, your Facebook page, your Twitter followers—is full of people who have not read all of your books. Or even most of them.

That's normal, too.

Fandoms are often specific to a single series. There are many, many points in a career where we need to start over for a lot of different reasons. At that point, our previously hot audience might be warm or even cool.

So we have a writer. Often an introvert, often lost in their stories, who from time to time lifts up their head and goes—oh shit, I should market my books.

- sends a newsletter
- books a promo blast
- discounts a title (or their publisher does it, maybe taking them by surprise)

We do these things because other people tell us to do them. Try Facebook ads, they say. Get a BookBub featured deal, Zoe says. (I do, it's true, but it's more complicated than that!)

What they don't say is, know who you're targeting. And how. And why.

THE TWO BEST AUDIENCES TO MARKET TO

A. your own organic list, collected as they read your books and you retain them
B. already warm-to-romance readers, collected in communities where book promotion is expected

I like to separate them so you can start to file away efforts under A or B, and realize when you might be a little mono-focused.

The Marketing Basics in Chapter Two? That's how you collect Audience A.

Other corners of the readerscape? That's how you find Audience B.

Both of these audiences can be reached a **low-cost**, *time-intensive* way, and both can be reached in a **low-time**, *higher-cost* way.

(It's hard to find marketing efforts that both take little time and cost nothing).

And then, once you have the hang of that, then you can also try marketing to the third audience:

C. cold readers, identified only by a loose connection to romance reading (having liked a Facebook page or using an Instagram hashtag about reading)

Understanding the difference between cold, luke-warm, warm, and hot readers is crucial to executing a smart marketing plan.

So, Cost Per Click (CPC) ads for example. They can be used to target cold audiences, or warm audiences. The campaigns would look quite different.

Know what your goal is, and work back from there.

Or pick something else that achieves the same goal.

If you're going to do that kind of ad campaign, to a cold audience to find new-to-you readers, you want ad copy that is about the customer, not you. Not even your books. Why this book is what *they* need, for *their* reasons. And sometimes the success of an ad campaign like that is less about cold audiences, and more about name recognition. (Not always! But sometimes).

So if you're starting something new: a new name, a new series—that's not the time to be betting the farm on a cold audience appeal.

One useful way to visualize this is a funnel. Here are two diagrams that show two potential reader funnel paths, although there are a lot of different ways this can go.

The Reader Funnel: From a Cold Audience to Fandom

First in series free   Word of mouth

CPC advertising on   Social media   network

a full priced book   exposure   bloggers

ONE SERIES

First in another   More books in that

series free **Warm Audience** first series

Launch of a new product

ANOTHER SERIES

Back catalogue   Social media

consumption **Fandom**   interaction

Adoption of

Fan art   characters/world

In the first diagram, we see a typical progression from cold audience marketing to collecting a warm audience from readers who have enjoyed those books, and then retargeting other series at them until a fandom develops on one or more of those product lines.

In the second, which is the outlier path we all secretly dream of but really can't plan for, it's worth noting that fandom doesn't extend to all future books. Even when a fandom develops off a single title, the commercial writer still needs to write more books. Even among outlier success stories, the (literally a) handful of authors who don't need to go on to write something else still need to go on to write something else, and it's never quite as well-received.

The writer's lot in life is to be humbled, over and over again. (What was I saying in the foreword about mental health? Yeah…)

The Outlier Success Path to Fandom

So (and in proofreading this book, I realized just how often I lean on *so* as a crutch word to show that I have A Point!, but we're going with it anyway, the joys of non-fiction and this is my voice…)

So, I say, now we have more context for the final parts of the bird's eye view of book marketing, and we realize they are, in their own way, the start of the cycle all over again.

A Bird's Eye View of Book Marketing

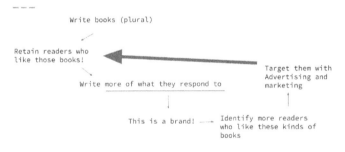

Write books (plural)

Retain readers who like those books!

Write more of what they respond to

Target them with Advertising and marketing

This is a brand! ⟶ Identify more readers who like these kinds of books

---

Homework: add another arrow to your diagram, and consider again if you have any reader retention strategies (the marketing basics from Chapter Two) still on a to-do list. We'll come back to that!

CHAPTER FIVE

SERIES 2.0, REVISITED

AT THE END of *Romance Your Brand*, I talk about Series 2.0, that second attempt at an idea that we really love. For me, this was Pine Harbour after Wardham, and then again, Kincaids of Pine Harbour after Pine Harbour.

It's refinement of a core story, a new series that carries forward almost all of your readers, and offers a new chance to draw in the readerscape that Series 1.0 hasn't quite appealed to.

[A note here: it's normal for books to be more niche than not. You haven't done anything wrong by writing books that have found some readers but not many; that is often the genre writing experience, because it is the genre reading experience. Readers are picky, and few books hit enough of our id points for us to give up our quest for the perfect book to deviate into a journey through an author's backlist. I hope, if you are a reader yourself, you can recognize yourself in that and be gentler on your expectations for your writing.]

In between writing Romance Your Brand and finishing writing this book, a global pandemic happened. And instead of going to writing conferences and retreats as planned, I dusted off my YouTube channel and made a few dozen writing and business craft related videos.

One of those was on Series 2.0, and you can watch it here: https://youtu.be/wP7zR02ccww

(Apologies to readers of the paperback version of this book, that's a rough link to type into a browser, but if you go to my YouTube channel, www.youtube.com/zoeyorkwrites and subscribe, then the Series 2.0 video should be pinned at the top when you refresh the page as a repeat visitor ... or just search for Zoe York Series 2.0, come on Zoe, give them the easy instruction first!)

I don't want to rehash the content in that video again for this chapter, so instead, I'm going to share some frequently asked questions I've received about Series 2.0 since releasing Romance Your Brand and following up with that video on YouTube.

These are inquiries I get over and over again, so if

you recognize yourself in them, know that you are in spectacular company.

Q: I don't like to write the same thing over and over again.

I'll forgive that this is not a question so much as an existential angst statement many can relate to. Is there a way to pivot the thinking on this to be more positive? There's nothing wrong with writing a lot of Series 1.0. I have written many of them. I will write more in the future. They aren't career *killers*, it's not that extreme.

Series 2.0 does a unique thing where it both reinforces your existing readership in a world and simultaneously improves on the cold sell to a new audience. When the right Series 2.0 comes to you, you will WANT to write it, because it will be new and exciting inside a world you've already created. This is not same-same, I promise.

And until then, you're writing a lot of different things and that's great, too!

Q: I changed the town/city/country my series is set in! Is that starting over?

Not at all, that definitely sounds like Series 2.0

material, because the "world" is in your case, literally a whole world, made up of different fictional countries. My first Series 2.0 was Pine Harbour, a different town four hours north of Wardham. "Same world" means there's crossover potential, the characters share the same world building rules, and readers will recognize the "space", thematically and emotionally, even if it's different.

Most setting-based series need to shift the "home base" a bit, just to give the reader (and writer) something new to explore! That's not the same thing as it being in entirely a new world.

Q: Can a spin-off series be a series 2.0?

It absolutely can, provided it reinvents the cast and world in a way that elevates the setting (as opposed to being smaller than, seeming derivative from the first series). In an UF series, for example, a Series 2.0 would be about a new protagonist on a big epic journey arc, just like Series 1.0 - it's not a set of side stories about the secondary characters from the first series.

I only say to avoid thinking about it as spin-off because you don't want it to be a derivative series from the first one, you want it to be bigger, better ... if anything, think about reverse engineering it so the first series can be read as a spin-off of the second. Does that make more sense?

Q: So, if a new series is set in the same world (one sweet/ the other sexy both country/small town) would a crossover book between the two work?

The crossover book should be in one series or the other, not a standalone book in between the two. But yes, definitely cross characters over! That's a great way to bridge between two series.

That being said, I think Series 2.0 is not going to be a *significantly* different heat level. That's just another Series 1.0 in the same world, which is good and fine and not a problem!

Q: I was wondering if you would do a series 2.0 with something that wasn't successful and didn't really ever find its readers? Or would you move on to something else and try to build some success there?

Yes, definitely if you have enthusiasm for a project, doing the same thing again with more intention, more commercial pre-planning, can be a great way to drive readers backwards to the first series.

If you keep pivoting, and trying Series 1.0 over and

over again, what if none of those find initial success? Sometimes success comes gradually, through fostering the tiniest of fandoms.

My final preamble-y thoughts about book marketing, and product design, is this:

Iteration is crucial for mastery

I first learned this precise version of a broader marketing principle (try, try again) from Skye Warren, who uses it in her Facebook Ads workshops and classes. But it's a lesson that applies to everything, and too often we stop before we've reached that mastery level.

This is a thought I'm going to come back to again and again throughout this book. Your plan is only going to get really tight, really sexy, and thoroughly romanced, if you try things over and over again. Iteration of reader engagement and iteration of an ad strategy, yes, but also iteration of storytelling, iteration of craft development.

We have stories inside us that want to be told, and they deserve our best efforts. They shouldn't suffer as only being our first attempts. If you look to the giants of genre fiction, who have long, lasting careers, you will find Series 1.0 attempts, and Series 2.0s that have taken their career to the next level. Just as we need the context of the bird's eye view of marketing, sometimes we need the context of a long-ranging career to clearly see with objectivity that iteration is key in our writing as well.

MASTERY CYCLE

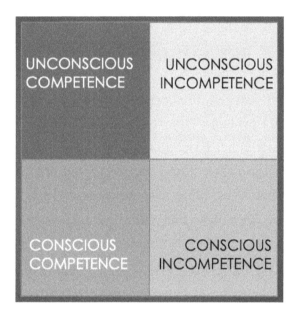

Before I wrote romance novels, I worked in medical education, and one of the tenets of any good training program is encouraging trainees to understand where they are in the mastery cycle (the four quadrants of which were first named by Noel Burch in the 1970s). When someone graduates from medical school, having mastered so much knowledge, they enter a residency program—and they're back at the start of the cycle again. And for many of them, their residency training program is just as long as medical school was in the first place.

We cannot rush ourselves to mastery. That's not how it works. We also should not shame ourselves for not being there yet. Ideally, we celebrate each milestone along the way, and when we decide to start over again—in a new genre, with a new pen name—we embrace the cycle anew.

Homework: Think about two different future projects you could map onto your bird's eye view of marketing template. One a Series 1.0, another a Series 2.0. Maybe use Post-It notes for this exercise, not committing to writing anything on the diagram itself until you think through the marketing pathways for one, and the other, and compare their utility to your plan, where you are in your career path. There is no right or wrong answer here, both can be quite useful.

PART TWO

ROMANCING
INDIVIDUAL ELEMENTS
OF YOUR PLAN

CHAPTER SIX

FINDING THOSE FIRST FIVE READERS, AND THEN BEYOND THAT

THE HARDEST PART of publishing is finding your first five readers. The second hardest is finding your first fifty readers.

And this is as true for a first time writer as it is for someone starting over again. So if you're feeling overwhelmed, I get it. I recently released my first French translations, and even knowing what I should do (bonjour, I'm writing a whole book about that topic), it still overwhelmed me and I threw my hands in the air.

So there's a reason I buried this chapter here, after laying out my philosophy about reader retention and the readerscape in part I. Because it's not just finding your first five readers. It's more that you get your first five **fans** by retaining five people who liked your book.

Don't just send review copies out there into a vacuum. Don't hope that those people will remember you 3-6 months down the road when you publish your second book (or book two in your next series).

Give them a chance to join your: mailing list, street team, review crew, fan club, private message board, or friend list on Goodreads/Facebook/Instagram/Twitter.

Retain as many readers as possible in a space where you can re-target them with subsequent releases

---

And because different people will want to be retained in different ways, this means having a mailing list, having a social media spot, etc. You don't need to manage your reader group on Facebook (although their group tool is really nice for that). Some people did really well growing a Yahoo group in the past, or a forum on their own website. Maybe it'll be Discord in the future.

The key here is moving beyond the stiff, formal communication and really connecting with readers (in a way that is comfortable for you: boundaries are important). What this looks like is really individual, but is some variation on you accepting the idea that you are a valued content producer that consumers will want a piece of.

Super awkward for an introvert, right?

Sorry about that.

Homework: How do your favourite authors interact with their fans?

Some examples I see: Kelley Armstrong is active on Tumblr, and does a lot of Q&As; Pamela Clare has a really tight-knit Facebook group; Jill Shalvis blogs almost every single day; Alisha Rai is active on Twitter (and in other gold star marketing examples, she leverages her Instagram and TikTok content across all three platforms).

What is your plan? What are you open to, and what terrifies you?

GOAL SETTING

My favourite question to ask an author is, "Five years from now, what do you want to have written?"

If you aren't pointed in that direction, fix what your immediate goals are. Re-align your current to-do list with actions that will get you to where you want to be way down the road.

But that long-term vision doesn't work for everyone —some people like to think about the past, building on what they've already accomplished. Others are rooted in the here and now, and are most interested in moving the needle immediately.

So play around with that question, and try some variations.

- Five years from now, what do you want to have written?
- A year ago, where did you want to be right now?
- Right now, if you sit with your secret thoughts, what is your most burning desire?

Those are all good questions, and I bet you can modify one of them to suit your own personality. Figure out the right touchstone question for yourself, and then turn it into a mantra. Elevate the question to a level where it has important meaning for you, and when you ask it, you stop what you're doing and really look at your goals.

Then, make sure the goals that follow from that

touchstone question are measurable. Some examples of metrics that I like:

- Five people in a reader group
- Fifty people signed up to an author newsletter
- One hundred units sold of book two after making book one free
- Five hundred pre-orders on the first book in Series 2.0

You can scale those numbers up and down, to be attainable and still a stretch from your current position. *This is your plan, not mine.* I'm only here to encourage you to romance it, to make it tighter and sexier, because that will get you closer to your end goals.

And then, once you set these measurable targets, you're going to do it again. Iteration. After five people join your reader group, your next goal is twenty.

Without a goal, you are less likely to take marketing action, and without marketing action, growth will slow.

There are times in our life when we need to let our fields lay fallow—when we're deep in the writing cave, when life gets rough. Don't stress about that. The marketing will be there when you are ready to dive in. But know that active marketing is a part of achieving your goals, and moving on from those first few metrics to the next level.

In Part I, some of your homework may have led to a to-do list. Over the next few chapters, we're going to dig into the individual components of a marketing plan and how we can romance each of them. Hopefully, as we dive deeper, some of the to-do list items will chunk up into more manageable, understandable steps—maybe for you to do, maybe for you to outsource—and on the other side you'll have a tight plan on the basics, and upon that, we'll start to build a monthly calendar for our book releases and sales events.

CHAPTER SEVEN

MAILING LISTS, NEWSLETTERS

AUTHORS OFTEN TALK about how important it is to **have a newsletter**. Other authors talk—mostly on Twitter—about how much they hate newsletters and never open them.

(This is not a personal attack, stop looking at me like that.)

You'll notice I sometimes use the term **mailing list** instead of a newsletter, and that's deliberate—I don't want to be limited to (or required to do) a monthly newsletter, and that's not usually how I structure my e-mails to my most interested fans.

Let's start with the basics. What is a **mailing list**? Well, at its most basic it's a list of anybody who's interested in what you do. Today, this means an e-mail list, although I supplement this with a physical mailing address list for holiday cards.

And because of spam laws, you can only accrue a mailing list of people who actually want to hear from you—so you'll need to use a mailing list service that does a confirmed opt-in process. (There are two different options here, confirmation on the original form or a double-opt in process; I've used both and I don't think one is better than the other, but double-opt in is more common, and is required in some countries, including mine.)

MailerLite
MailChimp
MadMimi
Active Campaign
AWeber
Constant Contact
iContact
FloDesk

These are just some of the services out there. I have had accounts at four of them, because the bigger my list gets, the more I run into problems with spam, etc. So I move my list around (it's *mine*, and I can do that, I just have to tell the new service how the list was built up [double-opt in via MailChimp, for example]). Most of them allow you a trial period, and some—including MailerLite and MailChimp, which are the two I recommend an absolute beginner start with—let you use the service for free until you hit a certain number of subscribers.

Okay, so that's what it is. Now let's talk about **how** I use it.

I use it to send people an email.

Simple, eh?

Sometimes I use newsletter templates provided by the company, but most of the time, I start the send out with, "Dear Readers," and let the words flow from there. I tell them about my new release, or an upcoming release, or a hot deal, or a friend's release. **I use it to send an email about something that I am genuinely sure my readers might be interested in**. I also, from time to time, write exclusive content for the newsletter (for example, a short story, a chapter at a time).

I collect these interested readers from my books. Front and back matter drive 80% of my newsletter subscriptions (and a lot of these come from my freebies). This tells me that my subscribers like me enough to want to hear more, but they're not necessarily super fans. **In fact, every time I send out an email highlight a backlist book, I sell a bunch of copies.** So there are *lots* of people on my list who haven't read any/many of my books.

Humbling. But also interesting, and useful information.

A few times a year I'll coordinate a freebie blast with a bunch of other romance authors, and we all send out a link to the blast on the same day. About half of those freebies soar into the top 100 free when we do that. **That's the power of mailing lists, and that's why I don't call them newsletters**. They're so much more than that, and also less — you don't need to collect formal bits of information to include all month long, you can just sit down and hammer out an email. And then send another one if you forgot something. That makes you human, and readers like the touch of reality.

Mailing lists are definitely in the "build it and they will come" category of foundational tools for an author. Push through the essential pain, open a MailerLite account, and get one set up. Everyone should have one. Mine sat very, very quietly for six months before I was in my first boxed set and got a bunch of new subscribers from that.

As we build a readership, engagement on that front increases. After eight years, I still get a thrill when I send out a newsletter and someone replies. That's lovely!

HOW OFTEN SHOULD YOU SEND AN EMAIL?

At least once a month, because you want your email address to stay current with the readers' email provider (Gmail, etc.). You want their inbox to recognize you as someone who sends them email! If you have a long pause of months, your next message is more likely to end up in spam.

So set a first goal for yourself of at least once a month (and I'll dig into what to send below). Once that becomes routine, then I'd challenge you to bump it to twice a month, and even more frequent around a release. Over time, you will see your open rate increase.

The key there is *over time*. Again, iteration is crucial to mastery. In September 2019 I took a workshop with Holly Mortimer of The Socialvert, who is an email marketing wizard, and she shared that fact about twice-a-month sending doubling an open rate. Something about how she said it really opened my mind to the possibility that I wasn't using my mailing lists to their full potential.

A year later, I can share that my open rates have moved from 22% to 33% on average.

It took a year. I'm not at the doubled level yet. *Yet.*

Iteration is crucial for mastery. What else did I learn over a year of consciously sending out emails more often? I learned not to stuff my emails with multiple bits of content. I learned a *lot* about subject lines (more on this below). And I learned that change is not always visible unless you zoom out to that bird's eye view.

I love a good year's retrospective analysis to see growth on measurable metrics!

WHAT DO YOU SEND IF YOU DON'T HAVE A NEW RELEASE?

If you don't have a sale or a new release to tell your readers about, here are three email ideas you are free to steal.

- First book in the series re-introduction
- A secret (truly make it surprising information!) about what's on your upcoming projects list; it doesn't matter if/when you actually write this thing! Just dangle it.
- A poll about how many books of yours they have read. *Make it anonymous*—I used SurveyMonkey when I did one recently. (And then whichever book has the lowest reads, that's your next sale/freebie).

Some of these points will give you very interesting

market research! In my recent reader survey, I used different collection links, so I was able to note the difference in responses from readers who I connect with on social media and those who are primarily on my newsletter. A couple of really fascinating takeaways from my survey were:

1. Common location (small town) increases read through over common theme (Navy SEALs or billionaire), even if the common theme has a higher initial one-click appeal.
2. Characters introduced in book 1 are more likely to have books read later on than characters introduced as the series unfolds.
3. I can close the gap in planning problems re: 1. and 2. with my social media readers, but it's much harder to close that gap with my newsletter subscribers. (*or*: there's work here to be done introducing them to those books! And there we go, more in-between-releases email content!)

But the final and easiest way to create more frequent emails is to take whatever you were going to jam into a monthly message, and give each of those valuable bits of information their own space in a weekly or bi-weekly message instead.

HOW DO YOU RECOVER A MAILING LIST THAT HAS LANGUISHED?

Start sending emails again.

I have done this! 2018 was a rough year for my family, and I may have only sent a handful of emails for Ainsley. I don't honestly remember. I do know that when I went to Holly Mortimer's workshop, both of my mailing lists were a little rough around the edges and dusty, too.

So the first thing you want to do is start sending emails again, just that simply. Then, you may want to consider re-engaging people who don't open the first few emails. (There are whole courses you can take to get really competent with email marketing, and I have a lot of Big Opinions about author-focused courses, but email marketing is probably one area where—if you are interested—a course is likely to pay off for you.)

A re-engagement campaign is done by first segmenting out the people who you want to target, then delivering them a series of emails designed to:

- give them something without asking for anything in return
- invest them in your journey (tell them a compelling personal narrative)
- get them to reply to your email (which trains their email provider that your address is a friendly, trusted one)
- see if they'll act on a specific call-to-action
- maybe find out what they are excited about (Navy SEALs vs Small Town romance, for example)

If the thought of creating a segment terrifies you, you can also run this type of a re-engagement campaign to your whole list. Treat this as yet another list of five email ideas, and between this and the list of three above, you have eight emails to send out already! Get them in the queue.

WHAT ELSE CAN I INCLUDE IN AN EMAIL?

- New releases.
- Sales on backlist books.
- Buy links, always.

- A look ahead at what is in the writing pipeline.

WHAT ARE SOME GOOD SUBJECT LINES?

This is constantly changing, and you'll need to do a bit of legwork for yourself to figure it out. Sign up for some author newletters. If you don't want to use your regular email address, create a throwaway test account. Personally, I like emojis, I like the word FREE, and I like questions. Oh, and my friend and co-writer Sadie Haller recently discovered that telling people it's your birthday is a great trigger to get them to open—and respond! Here are seven subject lines to get you started.

- Can I tell you a secret?
- Thank you!
- Meet [Protagonist]: dangerous, charming, and the hero of my next book
- 📚 Is this FREE book already on your Kindle or Kobo?
- This book is sizzling! Don't miss it! 🔥
- The countdown is on! 🧨
- It's official, we're splitting up

You want a subject line to grab eyeballs and create

questions, which will increase open rates! And then in order to keep reader satisfaction high, make sure the content inside the email answers the questions created by the subject line.

THE MOST IMPORTANT MAILING LIST HACK

As I mentioned earlier in this chapter, you own your mailing list. You can move it around from one service to another! (You should also back it up pretty often, just in case your service goes bust, but I wouldn't expect any of the ones I listed at the top of the chapter to be a problem in that regard.)

Here's the thing few people think about: what service you start out using isn't going to be the service you use forever. So from the beginning, or from right now going forward if you've already started publishing, I want you to start doing this: **Regardless of where you have your list, I recommend embedding your sign up form on a landing page you control, and/or using a redirect link, so the outward facing URL never has to change even if you change your service.**

My redirect link is:
www.smarturl.it/ZoeYorkNewsletter

I use SmartURL because it's a reliable service that allows me to change the original link under that link whenever I want.

Why do I suggest doing this? Because there are books out there with the raw MailChimp link in them, six years later, that people are just now opening up and reading. I know, because each month, I have a couple of newsletter sign ups at my now paused MailChimp account.

This way you can change where you list is growing without having to reformat your books.

Homework: If you don't already have a mailing list, create a MailerLite account. If you do have a mailing list, but you use the sign-up link your provider gives you, go and hide that under a SmartURL redirect link. I don't have affiliate codes for either service, I'm just a big fan of both.

CHAPTER EIGHT

SOCIAL MEDIA, A PREAMBLE AGAIN

SOCIAL MEDIA DOESN'T REALLY SELL books. And yet, it also *really* sells books. Often, it's a soft place for readers to land, and get invested in your brand, but every so often, it can be leveraged in a significant way to launch something new.

In short, it's a mess of contradictions, and also, for many of us, just a confusing mess.

If there's one secret to social media, it's that you have to really sink into using it for it to make a difference, which I laugh at a little, because isn't that true for everything? But social media in particular, I see a lot of people (including myself) trying something once, twice, maybe three times, and then throwing our hands up and saying it doesn't work. But if you think about building a brand awareness, creating content, nobody has a fandom after three attempts to establish that brand with a Facebook post or a Twitter thread.

Iteration is key. It's always key, but it's extra true here.

Social media is the ultimate in Build It And Then After a Long While They Will Come, Slowly and in Fits and Starts. Which means you must divorce yourself from immediate return on investment, you must be as objective as possible in deciding what content is working for your brand and when you want to change it up, and you must keep up a steady stream of it.

And, ideally, it shouldn't take much time at all.

In reality, it sucks many of us in, and leaves some of us frustrated, consumed by negative self-talk, and unable to write.

I have written and revised this chapter a dozen times since last year, when I first created this book file and started making notes on the essential elements of social media that directly connect to book marketing.

Social media is wild, you guys. It's complicated and problematic and a moving target in terms of what works. So it's hard to share best practices that literally change between final revisions and proofreading.

In our bird's eye view of marketing diagram, where email marketing is how we re-target warm audiences and cost-per-click advertising is the standard for engaging cold audiences (more on that to come in a later chapter), what is social media?

It's a chaotic mix of the two, and I think in part that's why it's overwhelming for many of us. It's all the things, all the time, without many boundaries or guidelines for best practices.

This is why I wanted to provide some context first, around cold and warm audiences, and how it's useful to document our Professional Endeavours—what we try and where we try it—as targeting new to us readers (cold) or retaining readers who have enjoyed our books (warm).

If you are wearing your author hat, you want to have a clear understanding of each task you give yourself.

Have I underlined that enough, now?

(Yes, Zoe, we get it, move on.)

One takeaway you can have from this chapter is that I don't want *you* to do social media. I want you to create an author persona, and I want you to do social media for that persona.

I have said before (in *Romance Your Brand*, and in some YouTube videos too) that you need to be your acquisitions editor to know which title you should carry forward to publication.

So perhaps in order to succeed at social media

management, you must be your own marketing director, coordinator, and assistant rolled into one. Or if you don't want to wear all those hats, you can budget a reasonable amount to outsource that effort. Time is money, and if you don't have money, then you need to put in the time. If you don't have time, money can get it done in a different way.

THE BASICS

There are lots of examples of authors who are not on one of the social media platforms (they're usually very good at at least one of the others, or they have a business framework that makes social media optional[1]).

As always, I'm not going to focus on the outlier examples. I'm going to talk about what are the basic best practices for any small business, and a genre fiction author is a small business owner.

Facebook is the most popular social media platform in the world. It also has a robust and affordable built-in advertising system. And the combination of personal profiles, business pages, and private groups make it an ideal platform to interact with readers.

In short, it's where people are. Up to 25% of all online activity takes place on Facebook. Like the reader-scape in general, Facebook is more massive than we can ever imagine—and a lot of the community interaction is private, inside groups, where we can't search. If something is happening on Twitter or Instagram, you can find it. Not true for Facebook. So if we're thinking about just understanding what social media is and how it works, know that Facebook is unique, and that privacy has some real advantages for readers. They can talk freely about what they like, and what they don't, for example.

The outlier example of how a book goes from a big release to a real fandom? That fandom happens on social media, and sometimes is exclusively because of Facebook.

So you want a Facebook account.

HOW CAN YOU USE FACEBOOK AS A WRITER?

At a minimum, you want a profile in your pen name, or one that's close enough, so you can interact with readers and other writers in groups (you can use a page for this, but you won't receive notifications in the same way, and it's not great for networking). Facebook used to crack down on "fake" accounts. Now they recognize that a pen name is a legit identity, but they still don't like too much flipping back and forth between accounts. If you have multiple accounts, set each one up on a different browser. Safari for Zoe, Firefox for Ainsley, etc.

You also want a page for your writing and/or pen name; this is like your website on Facebook. Passive branding. Also, where you can run ads through.

PEN NAMES, IDENTITY, PROOF, ETC.

If I were ever asked by Facebook to prove my identity, I would show them screen shots of my ISBN registration or publishing agreements, which have both names on it.

WHAT ELSE?

Each of the major social media sites attracts slightly different people. There are many different vectors along which you can plot the sites; I like to think of them in terms of a text-heavy to primarily-visual spectrum. How I place them on this spectrum is based on my own usage, research, and observation. Your perspective might be different, and I would love to hear how you would plot social media out on a line graph.

Whatever your metric is, plotting the sites out like this can be revealing for understanding which ones you like, and which ones you might want to try next, and where content can be re-purposed with ease.

Social Media Sites on a Text to Visual Spectrum

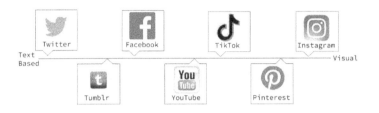

If you like Instagram, but you find Facebook too much, then maybe TikTok might be your thing. And if that works out, and you like creating videos…maybe you might want to expand into slightly longer videos for YouTube.

An interesting observation: TikTok accounts can directly link to Instagram and YouTube on your bio, but none of the other sites. That's probably because they see the connections there as advantageous to their platform.

You might be more comfortable on Twitter, and then making a leap to Instagram at the opposite end of the spectrum might be Not Your Thing. But Tumblr might be!

Although I think Instagram is a bit orderly, and the news feed is actually quite similar to Twitter. Maybe people who are drawn to a certain kind of input like them both? That would be another good line graph, how chaotic the different apps are. Versus Facebook and TikTok, where…good luck finding anything you randomly saw once.

Pinterest is hard to place on this graph in some ways because it's not exactly a social media site. It's more a massive search engine with a huge audience, but very pretty. This is social media meets CPC advertising. It's the second largest search engine in the world that Google doesn't own.

One downside of my line graph is that it doesn't centre Facebook right in the middle, but I blame the lack of Twitter-knock-off apps for balance. Because I really do think that, despite all the complicated and problematic elements to Facebook (which are myriad), it is where most book social media benefit can be found.

Whichever sites you choose to be active on, remember that there is a line between using it as a truly social activity (we all need more entertainment in our life!) and purposefully using it as a brand.

FACEBOOK: SURVIVAL MODE EDITION

One option for those who absolutely hate social media is to use it as if you are simply establishing an internet footprint, well-branded, in the same way you have a website. If you have a Facebook page, and the top post points to your newest or upcoming release, and the next post is about your newsletter—or YouTube channel, or release schedule, however you plan for readers to follow along with what you are doing—then you're ready for a lightning strike should it ever happen.

Those two posts could be it until your next release. In this model, social media is a search result information page, not an active source of reader engagement, and that's totally fine. Lots of brands don't actively engage on social media...but they do exist there.

GETTING FANCY: ADD A READER GROUP

But if you're willing to be more active on Facebook, I also recommend a reader group. It can be a lovely, calm place for you to interact with readers on your own terms, away from the chaotic noise of the Facebook news feed. You can make a group private (invite only), private but searchable, or open; I always recommend private but searchable, and include your pen name in the title. Like, "I Say, Sir: British Mysteries Author David Bridger's[2] Most Curious Reader Group". Or something.

And it's perfectly fine if you don't visit regularly. Just set that expectation up front, in the description on your page and in your group. "This is the reader group of

David Bridger, who really hates Facebook, but loves readers, so he pops in from time to time, between writing projects, to share sneak peeks at his latest crime scene. You might want to pour yourself a cup of tea, he might be a while."

OTHER READER GROUPS

If you've already got the page, the profile, and your own little corner of the Facebook universe, think about branching out and doing a group around your genre, or around a theme in your books. Or search out groups like that...but know that there are etiquette rules that are important to follow. If a group has author hosts...they're usually the only ones that can post. If a group is reader-driven, be a reader in that group.

If you want a group to promo in, start it yourself. Find similar authors and through a Facebook party to launch a new group. (Invite me to the party! I'll do some giveaways.)

WHICH OTHER SITES "SHOULD" I USE?

Should is such a loaded term! In the next chapter, I'll break down what to post on social media, and from that what, you might decide that you can use more platforms than you currently are...but honestly, as long as you have accessible information in one place, where other sites can point to, that's more than sufficient.

What you don't want to do is let anyone else snag your preferred author handle on Twitter just because you aren't using it.

I'm @zoeyorkwrites everywhere, for example. So whatever handle you use, consider creating an account at the various sites and apps. Stake the claim, and then you will have it should want to use it down the road.

TO END THIS CHAPTER, before I get to the actually good advice on how to re-purpose material from one marketing tool to another, I want to share an example of a recent attempt that didn't really work. Let's talk about a frustrating "failure" before we turn the page and launch into what I think works for social media.

One weekend not long ago, I shared the first chapter of my upcoming book all over the place. I shared it to my newsletter first, and then I posted it to my Facebook page. My newsletter's reaction to it was huge, a big surge in pre-orders. My Facebook page? Quiet response —maybe the super fans are already on the newsletter, maybe Facebook didn't show it to many people because of the length of the post, maybe I didn't sacrifice my offering to the social media Gods in the correct order. It doesn't matter the why, I don't need to over think it, just notice when something really takes off. Long excerpt: that's for the newsletter.

In that moment, I thought to myself, "What good is Facebook for anyway? I want people who have liked my page to see this chapter."

Insert foot-stomping and a significant pouty lip, too.

All I could see was This Did Not Work.

But when I thought about Facebook in a more holistic way, and broadened my general observations beyond that one post, I could see that my most successful post of that week was asking a single question: "Who loves Pinterest? Can I follow you there?"

In that question, I'm not asking for anything. Zero sales there. Just building connection.

That's what Facebook wants to be, a social platform. The more I use it as such, the more engagement I get, and *then*, I can get away with the occasional long-form book related post or direct sales attempt.

Otherwise, sales on Facebook are best funnelled through their ad platform (and a chapter on that is coming toward the end of Part II.)

The same is true for every other social media platform, too. Some authors will say that social media drives book sales, but I think that is selling themselves a bit short. Social media can be quite useful for building a platform, which you can then use to capture potential readers and funnel them toward a book.

That is not easy.

But we can try to make it a bit easier with a few shortcuts and some straightforward systems.

---

1. If you immediately skipped to the end to figure out how to opt out of social media completely, my best-guess outsider observer ideas are: actively pursue the outlier plan of selling a Hit Book at auction to a NY publisher; be an absolute monster at email marketing; write like the wind, and focus on production over promotion. So there are options! But they're all relatively extreme.
2. Author David Bridger was one of my beta participants when this material was taught in a single-run of a course in 2016. I like this reader group name so much I kept it in the book version.

CHAPTER NINE

BE YOUR OWN PR PERSON AND/OR OUTSOURCE IT!
DEALER'S CHOICE

ONE OF MY favourite writing business phrases comes from Becca Syme's Write Better Faster Academy: "QTP!" (Which stands for, "Question the Premise!")

So if you bought this book out of a serious sense of frustration that you can't get your marketing plan together, but you also maybe feel a searing resentment that you should even have a plan in the first place—why oh why do I have to?—I'm going to encourage you to QTP the idea that *you* should do XYZ from this book.

Probably somebody needs to! But does it need to be you? Or can you outsource some work?

A lot of resistance to outsourcing is the legitimate worry that someone else won't care enough, won't be invested enough, or won't know what to do. Other resistance comes from the cost of paying someone.

Before we dig in, let's talk about expertise. There are things one needs a specialist for; there are things any competent generalist can do; and there are rote admin tasks any assistant can do. Fairly, these levels of expertise have very different costs.

It helps to put tasks on a spectrum, with routine jobs at one end and custom jobs at another. The more fiddly it is, the more likely it is you'll need to do it yourself (or pay a specialist to do it).

There are tools we can build, and tools already built that we can pay for access to, that can move tasks from custom to more routine (for example, social media calendars for authors exist, and for a reasonable price, you can outsource the question of what to post, leaving only the…actually *posting it* part).

THE BASICS OF MANAGING AN AUTHOR'S SOCIAL MEDIA ACCOUNTS

Let's divide the work around generating this content into three stages: brand vision and design; write/create post content (graphic and text); post scheduling/submission.

The first stage of romancing your social media presence is figuring out your brand vision and design. You can work with a graphic designer to make a logo, set some brand colours, and either collect some selfies or get author headshots. Voila, an author brand kit.

(Zoe, it is not *voila, it is* hard *to get it right and actually look slick*!)

Iteration, again, is key. Try some different looks on.

It doesn't even need to be great to start, it just needs to be a thing. A photo of you. Your name in the same font as on your books (and if that's not the same mostly across the board, put that on your to-do list to fix, too).

Because if you have a brand kit, you can hand that over to someone and they can work with it. If you don't, then you're basically asking someone to start from scratch, and that's a heck of a lot more expensive without careful direction.

Let's call this, branding pre-work. If you want to DIY this with extra-ease, you can build a brand kit inside the free trial of Canva Pro, an online graphic design app that has a robust free version (I use the free version myself).

At the time of publication, this free trial is 30 days; I don't know what happens to your brand kit at the end of the 30 day trial if you cancel the Pro version, but you can re-create it easily in Google Drive, or literally in list form.

AUTHOR BRAND KIT

- name as a brand stamp
- secondary fonts
- signature colours
- optional logo
- examples of stock photo style

For example, my Zoe York author brand kit is:

- Trebuchet font for name, kerned[1] out
- Love Moon and Palatino serif fonts secondary
- Hot raspberry pink, with off-black accents
- no logo
- man chest and happy couple stock photos

But my Ainsley Booth author brand kit is:

- Avenir Next font, all lower-case for name
- Avenir Bold, various script fonts secondary
- Teal, black, grey
- no logo (series name in avenir ALL CAPS)
- black and white images, black backgrounds for embracing couples, high glamour, very sensual stock photos

Once you have this branding pre-work done, then you can practice using it to create some graphics. Again, iteration makes a huge difference here. Your first few teasers may not work. Your one hundredth teaser will be so much better than your first, keep going! The more you use the brand kit, the faster you will get at creating content that reflects your author identity in a single glance, which is the whole point: social media moves fast. You want your content to be instantly recognizable.

And as a reminder, that content can be systematized as well. At the top of the chapter I broke it down into five categories, and we're going to get to that in some detail shortly.

Logging in to social media to share something as your brand persona can feel a lot like staring at a blank page: daunting, confusing, intimidating. So I have two suggestions, and they're both rooted in the idea of being your own Public Relations Expert.

A PR person would not log in to your Facebook page and start building a post there from scratch. They would create a social media plan first, off-line, and then implement it.

"Create a social media plan" still sounds overwhelming, though, so let's break it down further than that. Once you have your brand kit, the next two stages are creating post content (graphic and text) and posting the content online (batch scheduled or live posting). If you can make some lists, of ideas and tasks, bound by the framework of your brand kit, that's a basic social media plan.

Two real game changers for creating social media content are using apps that have social media templates (Canva, for example, and Unfold is another that I really like for vertical layouts like Instagram Stories and TikTok) and using cloud-based storage to access those images, and also to jot down text ideas whenever they occur to you. I do mine in the Notes app on my computer, because it shares to my phone automatically, and keep lists of questions I can ask, email subject lines to try, and great lines from my books. Add your book covers to that cloud folder, and stacks of short links (a media kit for each book, basically), and **start building a swipe file**.

Social media gets easier when you get in the habit of:

- building a cloud bank of graphics and evergreen text
- re-using content in different ways and on different platforms
- Batch schedule everything you can
- Keep it simple (ABC): Ask a question; Book news; Content from your stories/world

Now we're getting to the part where you can do this yourself, or you can outsource it without too much expense. Also, you don't need to outsource something forever! You can hire a PA or VA or some teenager you know to help you get started and into a routine. An excellent screening interview question would be, "how many TikToks do you currently have in your drafts?"

If the answer is more than five, they're the kind of plan-ahead batch scheduler you need in your life.

And then you, or that TikTok savvy teen[2], can start to assemble *months* of social media posts.

Outsourcing (to yourself or others)

		Low Cost	Low Time	Pros and Cons
1	Author Brand Image	Selfies and cat pictures	Headshots	• Selfie options are easy (or a proxy for yourself, like a cat, dog, brand icon like a stuffed animal or cartoon emoji) - KEEP THIS LOW COST UNLESS YOU WANT TO SPLURGE
2	Consistent Graphics Set	DIY Canva	Outsource (Specialist)	• Many outsource options, including a mix of two (subscribing to a social media calendar that comes with Canva Templates) - EASY TO OUTSOURCE IF YOU AREN'T INTO IT
3	Post Content (Qs for engagement)	DIY List and Batch Schedule	Outsource (General)	• Time investment varies depending on skills with various platforms and comfort level with batch scheduling
4	Evergreen Book Related Content	Swipe File and Batch Schedule	Outsource (General or Specialist)	• Book posts are a combination of graphics, book content, links, call-to-action, and navigating the platforms; pros vs cons will follow from above
5	New Release Posts	DIY (Hinge on around release)	Outsource (Specialist)	• Author enthusiasm and insider information is key, so if you outsource, do it carefully to a specialist who can capture your voice

Divide the content into five categories to make sure you're balancing information for new readers and engagement for existing fans, both in an entertaining way that feels genuinely valuable: author brand image;

consistent graphics; reader engagement content; evergreen book-related content; and awareness campaigns around a new release or a sale.

And for each of those layers of content, understand that there is a DIY (low cost) and an outsourcing option (saves time, but varying expense). The more generalist the task, the easier it should be to find someone to help you do it at a reasonable investment.

For the DIY crowd, here's an example of what this might look like. Once a month, or once a quarter, spend a day planning something like this evergreen content example out. Then batch schedule a rotating cycle of social media posts based on it.

HOW TO RE-USE EVERGREEN CONTENT

1. Brainstorm a top five list of scenes from your books. *(Top five kisses, top five opposites attract moments, top five fight scenes)*
2. Blog that list! Don't forget buy links.
3. Use that list again to make a story for Instagram. I like the Unfold app or Canva to make the design part of the story dead simple. *(For Instagram, buy links can go in a LinkTree on your profile)*

4. Use that story again for Facebook! You can post it on your profile one day, and your page the next.

5. Share the blog post on Twitter.

6. Set a calendar reminder to yourself to share it again in a month, highlighting a different part of the list.

7. Take the same content and make a Facebook post with it, because Facebook prefers content be kept in-app[3]. **Don't forget buy links.**

Each time you do something like this, it goes into the evergreen swipe file for potential re-use. At first, you may not feel like you have a ton of content, but it quickly grows, and if you set a measurable, attainable goal, that will help.

How often should you post? Follow a schedule that feels authentic to you, based on analysis you think works for your corner of the readerscape. *I can't tell you what this schedule is. It's your plan.* ***But if right now you only post once a month or less on your Facebook page, you can up it, right?***

I have an active Facebook page for Zoe, and an inactive page for Ainsley. I will never judge another author for walking away from social media. I have done that so many times! It doesn't hurt your career. But if you put a bit of time and thoughtful planning into it, it just might help. (Same with Instagram, and all social media, really. I'm really present as Zoe, and less-so as Ainsley.)

HOW TO PLAN A NEW RELEASE OR LIMITED TIME SALE AWARENESS CAMPAIGN

This is the opposite of the evergreen content and reader engagement posts from above. When you have a new release or a limited time sale, the entire marketing plan can shift to focus on that event.

In Part III, I have a chapter on how to market a loss leader, which digs into the differences between pushing a free book and a 99 cent deal. That's the next level of a marketing plan, getting really nuanced with tailoring the plan to the product.

I see a lot of authors (and sometimes myself) not even giving new releases and limited time sales the basic treatment, let alone a nuanced approach.

Here is another place where outsourcing is a reasonable trade of money for time. Find an indie, genre-specific PR company to do a release blitz for you. Price can vary, but this is a few hours of work, so expect to pay between $80 and $400. I recommend, obviously, starting at the lower end of that range.

A release blitz should include a media kit for the book, some graphics, and a sign-up form for bloggers and reviewers, which they will also send to their own list. It is absolutely something one can DIY, but the truth is, many of us just aren't that organized or market-focused.

What a release blitz will not do is sell a ton of books. *That's not the point of it, at least not to my way of thinking.* I recommend them to authors who need some help getting organized around a release. You're paying for the framework. If you've invested $100 in a release blitz, you are going to get more organized around sending your newsletters, maybe. Make some graphics (or hire that out, too).

There is zero shame in building a team around you to get this done. That is good business sense if your business can afford it!

So if you just shook your head or groaned, know that you can outsource the writing of the newsletters, too. (This is a good use of a copywriter—hire them to batch write you six emails, which you can modify and tweak and use over and over again).

A smart release campaign is eight to twelve weeks long, starting six weeks before release, and extending two to six weeks after release (depending on when your next release is; if you only have two a year, stretch this campaign out longer). Holly Mortimer from The Socialvert does a mini course on how to prime your email marketing list for a release, and I have spent the last year iterating how to do the same on social media—this may sound wild because *gestures at the book you are reading*, but this kind of a sustained campaign does not come naturally to me!

I'm not great at marketing. I'm great at not giving up. At trying again, and figuring out what works a little, then doing that a bit better the next time. If you want to be your own PR person, that's all you need to commit to as well—or hire people who already have that winning mindset.

---

1. Kerning is a typesetting term that refers to the space between letters; it's a very common graphic design trick to increase the kerning on a name or title, beyond regular typeset, to make a word pop as more than body text.
2. Don't let a teenager post directly to your account without your permission. Just have them batch everything and then you can take a look. Teenagers aren't ready for the consequences of getting something awkwardly wrong, and your brand doesn't need the drama.
3. This is the error I made, in my anecdote at the end of the last chapter—I shared the first chapter of the upcoming book as a link to my blog. That might have worked if it was new and genuinely exciting for enough readers to let the algorithm know, this link is wanted. When I share a first chapter again, I'll share it in a more Facebook-friendly way.

CHAPTER TEN

WHEN YOU NEED A GET OFF THE GROUND PLAN

LET'S loop back to the baby author with a fanbase of five people, or the one with a newsletter of sixty subscribers. Who might be reading this section of the book and thinking, Zoe, I've done all of that. I have the website, I have the newsletter, the call-to-action is in my books. I even batch scheduled a lot of social media posts. And still…crickets.

I know, don't shout at me, but:

1. WRITE MORE BOOKS.

Write more books in that series. Write a long series. (This is the entire thesis of *Romance Your Brand*. A long series can be the difference between writing being a dream and writing being a career.)

And start a new series. Start over, but don't drift far. Write *your thing*, again. (That's Series 2.0!)

Those five people will turn into ten, then twenty, then fifty. I know. Fifty fans do not pay the bills. But don't abandon them, and their numbers will grow.

2. FIND PEOPLE WHO WRITE SIMILAR THINGS TO YOU. DO SOME THINGS TOGETHER.

Like what?

- Write a short story or a novella each, and bundle them together for a limited time 99 cent anthology that would appeal to all of your readers.
- Offer each others' first books to your core readers.
- Bundle your first in series together for a free anthology.
- Instagram hop.
- Interview each other!

A quick note on this: clear and transparent goals

matter. If everyone involved isn't interested in sharing their audiences, then they aren't the people for this kind of action.

3. ONCE YOU HAVE A BUNCH OF BOOKS IN A SERIES, MAKE THE FIRST ONE FREE.

If you are making nothing on a series right now—make the first book free. What's the worst that could happen?

4. ACTIVELY SEEK REVIEWS ON YOUR BOOKS.

Reviews are helpful for two reasons: social proof, and some advertising partners like them (like BookBub, a significant book marketing partner that I have mentioned a few times now, and will dig into in more detail in the Marketing a Loss Leader chapter). Reviews can also be hard to get at first (always!), so at the bottom of this chapter, I break down some of the different ways you can actively offer your books up to reviewers. Some have better success rates than others; some get you more quality reviews than others; some are better for a new release, etc. To maximize your number of reviews, it's not a bad idea to try a few of them.

Know the numbers: a good average for organic reviews is

one review for every fifty to a hundred paid sales, and one review for every thousand free giveaways through a retailer site.

5. GET SYSTEMATIC IN HOW YOU THINK ABOUT YOUR PRODUCT LINEUP.

I have a set of podcast episodes about this on The Sister-cast (look for the Marketing Breakout Sessions). And we're going to dig into this in Part III of this book, too.

6. WHEN YOU FIND NEW READERS THROUGH A NEW RELEASE, A CROSS PROMOTION, A SALE: INTRODUCE THEM TO YOUR BACKLIST.

- cycle your backlist through your social media in an appropriate way
- mailing list on boarding sequences
- backmatter in your books
- I can't harp enough on the fact that our newsletters are full of people who don't own all our books

There you go: six things you can do that don't cost a

lot of money, that find new readers, and expose them to your backlist.

More on using free as a marketing tool and cross-promotion with other authors in the next two chapters.

A SUMMARY OF BOOK REVIEW STRATEGIES

NetGalley

Primarily used by traditional publishers for ages, now indies can access this portals (at a cost) through co-ops. Most co-ops rent a month at a time, and that's all you need. You don't get a huge number of reviews from NetGalley, but the closer your series is to the middle of a genre, the better this experience will be, and if you get a couple of good quality "editorial reviews" from blogs, that's probably worth it. I find the ROI (return on investment) higher at the start of a series than later on.

Blog review tours

This is genre specific, and will be more successful if you pick a review tour company that regularly features books similar to yours. I've done them and had mixed results, but if you know your goals and pick the tour to match that goal, it's not a bad way to get reviews from bloggers. The best value here is reviews which have good pull quotes for the editorial review section for your books on Amazon (manage these through Author Central).

Goodreads — ARC offers

I started out as a Goodreads reader, so when I wrote my first (and second and third) books, I offered up ebook ARCs (advance review copies) in a couple of groups that had specific discussion threads for those offers. Since then, I've moved away from Goodreads because there are people there that hate read books, and I saw a lot of that with Hate F*@k (could have seen that coming, probably). But I still recommend it as a place to carefully source reviewers who are open to being solicited for reviews. You want to look for large reader groups that have discussion sections specifically for authors to offer up review copies—digital only! Don't mail paperbacks to reviewers, unless you have a deliberate strategy around like (like you're targeting bookstagrammers on Instagram).

Goodreads also has a paperback giveaway feature that they charge for—that is not the same thing as using

Goodreads to find readers who are actively looking for ARCs to read.

developing an ARC list of your own

This is where I'm at now. I have a google form, which you are welcome to copy: www. smarturl.it/ZoeYorkARCs

And anytime anyone asks about review copies, I get them to sign up. Notice that I ask them for a review before they join; I always have a free book, and they can download that and review it before getting on my ARC list. I get 30-75% compliance rate on an ARC send out.

ebook giveaways on social media

You can't require a review for a giveaway copy of a book, but you can offer ARCs up as giveaways before release, or as a regular giveaway afterward, and some of those readers will leave reviews. Volume makes a difference here in terms of how many reviews you net.

paperback giveaways on social media

This is more of a reward for loyal readers. I try to craft my giveaways in such a way that someone has to be familiar with my books to get a lot of entries, like I'll do trivia questions, that kind of thing. Because paperbacks are expensive!

CTA in the back of the book

This is the last point, because it's the most important. The moment when someone finishes your book, you have an opportunity to ask them to do something. Read the next book in the series, maybe, or leave a review for this one. You can say both of those things right after THE END, but only one can come first. (Also include a link to your email newsletter here!)

my newsletter. What a lot of smart authors do, who don't have ARC lists, is *they put a CTA that strongly encourages a review of book 1 — and offers book 2 free to anyone who does that.*

Homework: think about **what your goal is** with a book.

Remember when I told you that I wanted you to write the best book 1 you could imagine, and then make it free?

Now I want you to think about giving away the next one, too. **Why? Because this is how you build a loyal, invested reader base.**

It also means you need to have books 3 and 4 and 5 out. Don't pull the trigger on this marketing idea too soon! But if you set up the system just right, then you'll make more money on books 3-5 than you ever did on books 2-5, or 1-5.

And not everyone will write a review to get book 2. In fact, less than 10% will. So you're really only giving up a small number of sales there, in exchange for a steady, solid drip of reviews, and increased sales overall.

CHAPTER ELEVEN

MY FAVOURITE F WORD, AS A MARKETING STRATEGY

HOW DOES Free fit in your marketing strategy? How do you maximize its role?

This slides back to the idea that your product design —series length, for example—is an essential consideration in a long ranging marketing plan. Marketing is not just what you do after the book is done and in the vault, it starts with considering what you will produce in the first place.

Free fits into a marketing strategy for a long series. Three books at a minimum, ideally five or more, full-length novels at full price. But let's get a bit more specific here about those books.

YOU WANT THEM TO HOOK INTO EACH OTHER

Cliffhangers? Teases? Whatever you want to call it, I want the last scene in book one to create questions in the reader's mind about book two. If you are self-published, you can go back and layer this in to previously released books without anyone noticing. A few sentences is all it takes.

YOU WANT THEM TO BE AS CONSISTENT AS POSSIBLE

Trope-y book one? Make book two equally trope-y, so you've hooked readers with more of the same. Again, you can go back and fix this, but it's harder than just adding a few sentences at the end. This is a Series 2.0 goal.

Similar length. Got a short book? Fix it with a long epilogue! (Call it bonus content and do a promo push while it's still paid, or if it's later in the series, on an off month to when you are pushing the freebie)

Pick another book in your series, later in the series, and make sure it works as a "monster of the week" or standalone series entry point, too, and representative of your best work. That could be a future free deal!

YOU WANT TO THINK ABOUT YOUR CALENDAR FOR THE YEAR

I very loosely plan twelve months out, knowing that it can change in an instant — but when the plan changes, the first thing I do is wipe the slate clean and plan the next twelve months again. I do this on the back of an envelope most of the time, very rough. But in the next section, we're going to get very detailed on how to do this in a systematic way.

A FREE FIRST IN SERIES IS A GOOD HOOK FOR A COLD AUDIENCE

This free first in series is a very good place to try your hand at cost per click advertising, to regularly try new email blast deals, to use for cross-promotional purposes.

AND THEN YOU DO IT ALL OVER AGAIN

Do it again with another series. You can hammer a single series to death with marketing efforts, but if the market doesn't respond, move on and try the same techniques on a different set of books. This doesn't mean you're abandoning that first series *forever*. Book trends are cyclical, and I have had series bounce back after being on hiatus or laying fallow for quite some time.

But I also want you to move forward and apply all of this to a new series, too. In *Romance Your Brand* I talk about some of the amazing advice I got before I hit publish, and how it shaped me as a genre fiction author. One of those was a conversation about "what is the best book you've ever written", and Kate Pearce — an absolute legend — said she hadn't written it yet.

That was almost ten years ago, and I bet she would say the same thing today. So would I, after fifty-something books. My best work is still to come and so is yours. Do not get stuck in trying to make your past work connect with an audience at the price of not producing new work, which will be better, tighter, and more on brand.

To recap: free works in a meta-data connected series of similar books; in order to maximize it's efficiency, you want to plan out a new free price drop a month or two before a new release (depending on how busy your calendar is), and consider using later-in-series books as free hooks. Between two new releases, a first in series free, and a later in a series free, you have four events for a year for a single series, and that's before we consider anything else, like a cross promo event, a re-brand, or a boxed set release.

The best marketing plans have layers. Like onions, and romance heroes.

Homework: Make a list of your series, and highlight which books would make good loss leaders to hook readers into reading more of your books. Think about which of those books actually have a hard tease for the next book in the series, and which might need a tiny bit of polish in that area.

CHAPTER TWELVE

CROSS PROMOTION

ALMOST EVERYTHING I suggest can be done solo. I was the kid in school who hated group projects! I get nerves about wanting to rely on others, because of high standards or concern about burden of work. There are lots of writers who work that way, to protect their brand, or because they aren't sure how to approach potential collaborators.

If you are resistant to networking and cross-promotion, it might sound something like this:

- I can't recommend a book to my readers if I haven't read it and loved it
- I don't know if I want to associate my (filthy

dirty smutfest) with someone else's (sweet as sugar pie joyfest)
- I don't want people to unsubscribe from my newsletter if I send them more than the bare minimum I promised I'd send them
- I can't spare the writing time on chatter

When you read it as I've written it out, does it sound negative? Sometimes we throw up brittle barriers because they feel safe, but they can also block us from opportunity.

Reframe your narrative, and set boundaries instead of barriers.

- I can make time for **value-added promotions** that my readers will appreciate. (and it's okay if I pass on anything else)
- I **do** want to collaborate with (this type of writer)
- I **do** want to grow a mailing list of people who **want to receive email** from me; and I want to send them **value-added content** they are likely to appreciate
- I can spare 15 minutes a day for business talk, and **I'm going to make it count**

Boundaries are healthy. But so are connections, and they don't get forged in a vacuum sealed by negativity.

All of the stuff I've shared so far: writing a series, hanging on to my readers, making the first book free...all of that has solidified my foundation. But each advancement in my career, except maybe writing my premium brand series, has been because of a collaborative project that was borne from networking.

2013: A writer friend I made on Twitter asked me to put my first book, that no more than seventy people had bought, in a boxed set that Christmas. That boxed set, *Love for the Holidays*, took me from five readers to five hundred, and it earned me enough money to pay for my first BookBub featured deal in early 2014.

2014: Thanks to a thread in an online writing forum (Romance Divas), I wrote my first military romance for the SEALs of Summer boxed set. That release took my reader base from 500 to 1000, hit the bestselling lists (#6 on the New York Times combined list, #22 on the USA Today list in the first week, *and lingered on the USAT list for another three weeks!*), and gave me the courage to try and do this full-time. (Which was in turn the impetus for creating Pine Harbour, which is the first series I crafted with intent, so see? That's because of networking, too.)

2015: Well, technically this started at Christmas

2014, but it was right at the end of the year. I built a Facebook group of authors completely dedicated to freebie blasts. No chatter, no promo, nothing but...if you've got a free book, and you're willing to send out a newsletter, you can put it on this list of ALL THE FREE BOOKS. Our readers loved it. Six years later, and we're still running these free blasts. Each one just as strong as the last. Out of the box thinking that wasn't a drain on ANYONE. Valuable content for readers, worth the effort for authors, win win win.

2016: I did some shared world series. These come with a potential reduced total income for a book, but hopefully the cross-marketing means you find new readers for your other series. Worth the try.

2017: I wrote a story for a unique anthology idea, where we all wrote to the same blurb. That collection, *Love in Transit,* is now a paperback collector's item at book signings, and three years later, I still get asked to sign it at events.

2018: I worked with two of the authors from *Love for the Holidays*, my very first collection, to do a five-year anniversary special release: *Snowed in for Christmas*. We each wrote a novella, and the set debuted on the USA Today list. Worth noting here: Love for the Holidays did not hit a list when we released it in 2013. Iteration is key. Try, try again.

And I'm keeping my eyes open for other opportunities, too. I'll admit, I'm getting tired. It's been a busy few years. So there's pacing, too. And writing. But I need to keep the perspective that I wouldn't be in this position right now if it wasn't for the network of authors that's helped me get here. There's some paying it forward that I need to do, too.

HOMEWORK, if you want it: Come up with a positive mission statement for networking and cross promotion. What's your goal for the next year?

CHAPTER THIRTEEN

BORROWING GOOD MARKETING IDEAS

VERY FEW OF my ideas are original. Newsletter serial? Cross-promo freebie blast? Small town military romance series with trope-y hooks? All borrowed from people I admire.

Some people are reluctant to **copy**. Don't copy. See how simple that is?

When you see a good idea, **absorb it.** Let it roll around inside you until you feel it from the inside out, until it's 3D and *yours*, and then when you implement it, it'll be different enough to be yours and not a carbon copy of someone else's.

Nobody really gets ahead by being a carbon copy. Because there's someone else out there that's doing it more authentically.

But it's hard to forge a completely new path, too, and why should you, when the proven track is already laid in front of you?

Think of the successful authors you've observed over your career. Some of them are true trailblazers, but many are not. Many have been called "the next _____". Think about why that feels like a fair, authentic label. Because they ARE like that first author, but they're also a bit different. Maybe even better. Fresher. More modern. But familiar.

Figuring out this ^^^^ is the first step to taking your career to the next level. You want to be the next _____, right? (And it's okay if the name _____ isn't Nora Roberts. I shudder at the thought of carrying that much weight on my shoulders. But I'd love to be the next Jill Shalvis or Robyn Carr). It's also okay if the name isn't a name, but a tight market focus. I think of people like Theodora Taylor, Susan Stoker, and Lucy Score, who all know exactly what they are going to write and do not deviate from that plan.

Some of us don't like to stick to a plan for long, and it's absolutely okay for careers to flow from one genre to the next. If our goal is to have some book-selling success, though, shouldn't we give each of those genres a fighting chance before we move on? Absorb that, too.

Everything needs to be blueprinted to a goal. I'm

doing X because of Y. In this case, I'm committing to a marketing plan to reach new readers. Reaching new readers is important to me, and this is how I do it.

That's a bit rambly, but sometimes that's what goal-setting is like ... talking it out until you stumble upon what really matters, what your key goal is.

CHAPTER FOURTEEN

BRAND RE-VAMPING

BRAND RE-VAMPING CAN HAPPEN on an entire catalogue level (like splitting different genres out to
different pen names, or absorbing backlist into a new,
more successful pen name), or it can happen for a single
series.

WHEN TO REBRAND A SERIES

- If your covers have fallen out of sync with
  what is current for your genre
- If your branding has been tested in the
  markets you have access to and reception
  wasn't where you wanted it to be

- If your branding has run its course in the markets you have access to, and you want to re-position a series for a different segment of the readerscape
- When you can afford the investment (of either time or money)

The final point is the most important, and I want to expand on it a bit. If the thought of paying for new covers on a series makes you feel a bit nauseous, then it's not time to do that, full stop.

There are other ways to advance your marketing plan. Put this on a goal list. Don't forget about it. But raise the money for it through other marketing efforts first (and those might be, creating more product and pushing that, then leveraging those funds backwards to bring the backlist along for the ride).

I feel the same about cost-per-click advertising, which I have put off discussing until this point in the book (although the time has come, that's the next chapter). Brand re-vamping and CPC advertising are both low-time, high-cost marketing strategies.

If you are not there yet, you need to focus your plan on high-time, low-cost strategies instead. Sometimes it takes money to make money. This hits differently for authors of varying privilege. It hits differently for single authors who don't have a partner to share household and life expenses with. It hits differently for authors who come to writing while in poverty, with bills that aren't going anywhere any time soon.

I know that, and I'll say this: if you are at the end of your rope, and you know you need a brand re-vamp and you cannot afford it, email me, and I'll help you. I make all my own covers. If you like them, and you need something along the lines of my ability, I can make you a set of covers for a backlist series.

But I can also maybe connect you with affordable cover artists, or help you figure out how to make your own covers, too. That option isn't for everyone, but maybe there is someone relatively in-house to you who could help: a critique partner, a spouse, a sibling, a child, a best friend, or a part-time personal assistant. (Some of these people will want to be paid, some will want to barter, and I'm a big fan of compensating people more than fairly. Don't be a taker!)

Bringing branding work in-house helps in more ways than just saving money. It also you to be more flexible, to try out a new design idea without a significant commitment, and it helps you test the marketplace through Facebook ad graphics, website design, teaser images, and boxed set bundles.

Plus today there are more tools than ever before to

make this relatively easy for a dabbler. (That being said, and I said this in *Romance Your Brand* as well, DIY covers need to be absolutely professional, and you need to know there are as many revisions for a cover as there are for a book. Maybe more.)

One key takeaway from the bird's eye view of marketing is that brand is created in the marketplace; without that market response, it's simply an attempt at a brand. (This is such valuable learning, though, may we all learn from our New Cokes)

Your idea of what your brand is may not be what readers see or think after reading your books. I want to repeat that:

Brand is created in the marketplace

Don't invest so heavily in packaging that you won't toss them if/when they don't work to meet your marketing goals. Book covers are product packaging, and product packaging needs to be tested in the market.

We need to normalize the books get re-packaged as part of a marketing plan, and we need to support each other in finding affordable ways to get that done.

CHAPTER FIFTEEN

CPC ADVERTISING

YOU AREN'T GOING to learn enough to go from "Facebook ads don't work" to "sweet, a 10x return on investment!" from this chapter.

I'm not that good at running cost-per-click advertising myself. It's not a natural fit for my strengths, and I don't really find them that interesting.

But—they do work, and when we get our business clicking along nicely, they are one of the most accessible ways to level up.

For most people, especially anyone who is anxious about spending money on their author biz, that time is later in the marketing plan than they think it might be.

As I said about social media, there are outliers who make me look foolish for saying that, but they aren't reading this book, looking for some help in making sense of ad campaigns. They're good.

Here's what I have learned about this type of marketing: cold ads convert when you have **the right product** and the **right ad copy**.

The right ad copy will not sell the wrong product. The right product will not sell itself with the wrong ad copy. And figuring out which is wrong (or maybe, is it both?) is very hard to objectively ascertain when you are the creator of the product.

So Facebook ads (and any other CPC mechanism, but for most authors, this is the one to use) is not a machine that can be studied, analyzed, and then **taught to someone else** to use **reliably**.

What can be taught (or, from our perspective, learnt) is the process.

Which is, no surprise, iteration. It's literally Skye Warren's word for ads, and she is the one to listen to on this topic, not me.

But iteration requires investment. Here's the hardest part—most people are testing ads at the limit of their comfort level, when the next thing to do after testing an ad is to scale it up.

So the people who do really well in ads have a nest egg to play with that really helps. [So my very conservative advice is, save up for this, and write the whole thing off as a learning experience and a business investment before you even begin.]

It's the same as gambling. People who are really good at gambling can afford to lose, and they're disciplined about those losses. You can ride a high for too long, thinking you've figured out the machine this time.

You haven't, because there's no machine. The skill is in reading the odds.

And you don't even have to test ads to start analyzing *the product*, which is half of the equation.

What are the odds of a marriage in trouble book being a good small town series starter, Zoe?

The best small town series starter is someone returns to the small town after being away for a while and falls back in love with it: if that's not your small town book one, you're not playing the right game, and ads won't help you.

(Obviously, by you, I mean me, welcome to my therapy session)

So people who do really well at ads in publishing are nailing the product first, both in production, but also in selection of a product to promote via cold ads.

Do not beat yourself up if you have not nailed the product! It is hard to do this. I struggle with doing this! And I have a successful career even though I struggle to do this.

Here's a truth bomb:

Nobody is doing well pushing an off-brand product.
Nobody.

What do I mean by off-brand? If brand is created in the marketplace, then this is the example of a product pitch that is a miss for the target audience. If your ad copy and product don't match: that's off-brand.

But also, literally any low-concept book is off-brand for the *cold* audience of a Facebook target market (because the audience needs to know in a split second what it is).

You cannot sell low-concept books with CPC advertising as a standalone product. It doesn't work. Books like that get sold through hooking on the author's general brand, other books, or as a loss leader to a warm audience (for example, a BookBub Featured Deal sells a low-concept book so much better than a Facebook ad does; you have longer with the reader's eyeball, and there's a tacit endorsement from the editorial selection.) And that is an equally valid marketing technique. Ads might work here to a free first in series, marginally better, maybe enough to break even, but it's not the ideal product to practice one's iteration on. If a book doesn't sell at full-price, it's not the right product. Any CPC ad that lands on a product that costs money, the product must sell itself.

And the book? Either free or full-price. Never 99 cents.

The math doesn't work on a 99 cent book. There is almost no way to make a 99 cent product that you earn maybe 35 cents on (or less if you're with a publisher) profitable using a cost-per-click ad model.

The people who do it are making the money elsewhere.

Sure, some people can get that CPC down to a glorious <10 cents, but then 1/3 clicks must convert to a sale to break even, and that's not great odds. The ROI (return on investment) is dodgy as heck.

So that's the product side of the equation: from my entire backlist of fifty-something books, I have been able to easily set up Facebook ads on five of those books.

Five.

All others that I have tried have been a struggle that I started to recognize over time. Each one , not the right product.

That's okay! You only need one or two entries into your catalogue to run ads on, when you get to that level. Better to know all of this while you're working on revising and expanding your catalogue, too.

On the other side of the equation is the right ad

copy. This is a lot like email marketing, where you will want to watch the market, watch your corners of the readerscape, and start to build a list of examples, of language that works.

Cold sales should be about the audience. What is in it for them. Think of adjectives like un-put-down-able, heartwarming, page-turning. Price motivators like free and borrow in Kindle Unlimited or Kobo Plus.

And dig around in the Facebook Ad Library (www.-facebook.com/ads/library/). You can search for authors by name (start with me, I might have an ad running), and see what they are trying out. Don't copy the styling of the first author you look at. Get a wide cross-section of what people are trying, see what ranks their books have, and do some careful analysis to pull out language that may be helpful.

I'll repeat what I said at the top. Cold ads convert when you have **the right product** and the **right ad copy**. Don't lose sight of that, and when the time is right, you'll be able to add an ad campaign to your promotional calendar.

CHAPTER SIXTEEN

WEATHERING THE LOW POINTS

WHEN I WAS A KID, my mom told me something about life happening in seven year cycles. I wish she were still alive so I could ask her about it again, and provide a fulsome preface to what I'm about to say, but she's not, so I'm going to launch straight into a random theory.

What if there are three stages to being a commercial genre fiction author?

Stage one: discovery and puppy-like enthusiasm
Stage two: drudge work, self-doubt
stage three: mature career

And what if each stage was, with some significant give or take, about seven years?

When I was a young author, I had a number of metrics fixed in my mind: I needed to write in a series, with at least five books in it, so I could make the first one free; I wanted to write ten books by the end of my second year of writing full time, and aim for thirty in order to make full-time money off my backlist.

And then, I was quite sure, I would be set on a decent path of hard work and lovely reward.

I did not account for a global pandemic. Or a husband with profound PTSD. Or, in addition to both of those things, just hitting a wall seven years into this career. Life comes at you fast when you think you've got it all sorted out, and sometimes when you don't, too.

The thing is, any earlier in my career than right now, if I read those three stages as described, I'd think...yeah, makes sense, and i've looped through all of them already.

Because the sophomore book is often so much harder than the debut, so you feel like you've gone through that doubt cycle and come out the other side more confident. And my period of puppy-like enthusiasm didn't last that long, I tell myself, because I had a pretty slow start until I found some cross-promotional opportunities with other authors. I had all the self-doubt in the world back in 2013. So what followed, a slow, steady climb into success—that was the mature career, wasn't it?

But this is a trap, thinking that as good as we can get it in the first five years, that's as good as it will ever be. That's not the Mastery Cycle. One mastery cycle just spins into another, and we're always starting over again, but there's something about that sophomore run through it that is a real struggle.

Right now, I'm just figuring out what I don't know. It's a precarious time, and a weird one to be writing this book in, lemme tell you that.

But every single author who has been in this 30 years has gone through this cycle in one way or another.

I first started to think about this theory because someone said, "Nora Roberts and Brenda Jackson all write really long series. Why do you say end a series between 5 and 8 books?"

[First of all, if you are having a really great time writing a super long series, don't end it because I think you could do better with Series 2.0—I might be wrong, and making hay while the sun shines is a better rule than randomly listening to me.]

But if you look at the career arc of those authors, their really long series were launched at the start of the third stage of their careers.

At a conference I attended last year, a very successful

author published by big New York houses shared that she had recently signed to a new agent. Her third, she said, and maybe there was something to be learned from that. Maybe all authors go through three agents in their careers.

Or maybe we're just drawn to rules of three, I don't want to overstep and connect what she was saying that firmly to my theory. [But it makes sense, a different agent for each stage, because the goals are different.]

As a self-published author, I am my own acquisitions editor, my own agent, and here's the secret downside to that: it's hard to dream big. I don't have that external partner saying, "I believe in you."

[If that's you, too: I really do believe in you, and I know you believe in me, and we should tell each other that more often.]

What did my drought look like? A dramatic drop in word production, fatigue around marketing, and an unexpected disconnect from the hungry ideas of my earlier writing days.

I mask it well, and this is my job, so I still do what I need to do—but right now, writing is very much a job. And when people ask me if I want in on things (those cross-promotion ideas I was so game for from 2013 through to 2018), the answer is almost always no.

It's a retreat to just writing, basically. And there's

nothing wrong with that! Because I have writing friends who have been doing this a lot longer than me, I know this is normal. It's a period of reflection and regrouping.

The hardest thing to consider is that it might take a while to come out of—I don't like that idea at all. I don't want a seven year drought on enthusiasm!

But I don't think it's actually that simple. Of course there will be blips of eager ideas in there. They just might be harder to grab on to. People keep working and writing during this fallow period, it's just at a different pace than before. And *if we stick with it*, we will one day realize that the words are pouring out of us again.

This is true for the cyclical struggles of a long career, and it is true for more personal, acute periods of stress. Be kind to yourself. Be gentle. And most of all—maybe hardest of all—be patient. And keep writing, in fits and starts if you need to, but keep a toe in the game. One day, the words and the ideas will return.

PART THREE

PLANNING TEMPLATES
AND EXAMPLES

CHAPTER SEVENTEEN

PLANNING YOUR MARKETING CALENDAR

EVERY WRITING CAREER will have ups and downs, and there will be stretches of time without new releases. In this final part of the book, we will discuss what a year-long plan could look like for you and your backlist.

One of the hardest lessons I had to learn in publishing is that changes made today have the biggest effect months or even years down the road. I am not a patient person! And this is frustrating when starting out and feeling the financial pinch of investing or waiting.

But over time, if you are able to plan ahead to have releases or marketing events at consistent intervals, that shift income concerns (and maybe freakouts over lack of sales) away from the present (which is done and already decided) to the future, where you don't need to freak out because change is within your control. **This is where the marketing calendar tool comes into play, breaking up the monolithic task of book marketing into manageable chunks.**

You can download a .pdf of this marketing worksheet from my website at:

www.romanceyourbrand.com/worksheets

If you have releases planned over the next year, that's awesome. They are going to be highlights on your calendar. If you don't, or you only have one or two, that's okay! The rest of your calendar is *wide open* for marketing awesomeness. The next year may be where you are going to focus on revitalizing, promoting, and maximizing your backlist titles.

[If you don't have a backlist yet, then the next year should be about, in addition to getting a few releases out, **planning a future backlist**. Front list, aka new releases, only last for so long. Pretty soon, everything is backlist. How do you want it to operate at that point?]

HOW TO USE THE WORKSHEET

1. Think about each series as a horizontal line. If you have more than three series, subdivide horizontally now, giving yourself up to 6. More than 6 series? Use two sheets.

2. Plot release dates first. I don't worry so much about balancing these over the year, because another marketing event is just as good as a release, and you'll be balanced in the end.

3. Look at the gaps both horizontally (across a series) and vertically (across your brand).

4. Fill in gaps, ideally in a balanced way, with marketing events:

- Horizontally, try to pick a mid-point between two releases for a marketing event (or two events at the 1/3 and 2/3 points if you have a long gap). This keeps your series visible in the steadiest way. If this isn't possible because of vertical balance (see b), then shimmy a marketing event closer to the next release by a month or two.

- Keep filling events in across series until you have at least one marketing event in each month vertically, giving your brand a boost at least once every 4-6 weeks.

The more books you have, the more likely you will be to run separate calendars. I suggest separate marketing schedules for:

- different pen names
- very long series that are a world unto themselves
- off-brand books (build a routine with readers for this over the years! I do a little push every April Fool's Day for my off-brand Vikings in Space series, which I re-brand for a single day under the pen name ZORK)

Additional things to consider when planning out a year:

- Pre-release ramp up
- Post-release focus (extend that front list period as long as possible!)
- Low and high sales months
- Momentum
- planning ahead for a known break in the release schedule

This tool is a great way to get yourself back on track

and recover from an unexpected bump off course. If you have enough of a backlist, you could even plan out an entire year of promotion using this method, and get back into reader visibility without writing new words.

If you think about each marketing basic idea (a free book, a newsletter campaign, a CPC ad campaign) as a thing to try in a month, and each idea could be repeated at least once per year, then you only need six decent marketing ideas to get you through a year without a new release. Here is a list like that, although I bet you can make an even smarter list of your own, that is tailor-made for your own plan.

INITIAL MARKETING TO-DO LIST SUGGESTIONS

- first in series free
- cross-promotion with similar authors
- newletter campaigns (bonus content, backlist promotion, re-engagement)
- re-packaging
- later in series free
- a focused CPC ad campaign

If you already made a list of which books in your

catalogue would make good free loss leaders, and which books need to be re-packaged, and have an idea or a goal around cross-promotion, then you're half-way to having a year's worth of calendar content already.

INSTRUCTIONS /

months along the top, starting with next month;

series/project groups down the side, sub-divide horizontally as needed

TO-DO LIST SUGGESTIONS /

first in series free

later in series free

series bundles

newsletter campaigns (bonus content, backlist promotion, re-engagement)

re packaging

___

CHAPTER EIGHTEEN

ROMANCE YOUR YEAR (OR MONTH, OR QUARTER)

NOW WE HAVE a list of marketing ideas, and a few new releases. Is there an ideal way to plan those out over a year? What does a rock solid year-long marketing plan look like? And what does it look like if we need to plan quarterly (because we don't have that many titles) or we have a good sized backlist, but we won't have many releases, because we're in a slump?

A ROCK SOLID YEAR

The principle here that is that if a book event drives sales every month, income will be steady and maybe even grow as the brand (relatively passively) collects new readers. For example, a new release, backlist free push, an ad strategy kicking in, or a newsletter push. Since there are four things there, you would cycle through them all three times, if used equally. Which means at least 3 releases in a year to keep momentum going, and the more you can layer these things up, the more solid the year will be. Let's aim for four releases in a year, to be lofty in our goals. This is also nice because a lot of business talk breaks goals and metrics down to quarters. ("What's the Q1 plan for 2021?")

If a year is too much, let's get granular.

WHAT WOULD AN INCOME-CHANGING MONTH BE?

My best income months are consistently ones where I have a book release that readers are looking forward to, and I have a BookBub featured deal on a backlist book for free, one that's part of a series. That combination is reliably a good income lift, but usually, I like to spread those events out, because I don't like to leave the months on either side bereft of my best income ideas. But for someone who is balancing a seasonally heavy day-job, like an accountant, a teacher, or a retail worker who pulls overtime around the holidays, then steady months may be asking too much.

A KILLER QUARTER

One or two good quarters in a year can carry slow months when we're focused on other things. You can pare down the year-long plan to a single three-month period, and try to get three things in back-to-back:

- a re-brand with a sale push (coordinated, re-brand and then free first in series in month 1)
- having a book done far enough in advance to book promo for the release in month 2 (and be comprehensive about that promo, full court press)
- make month 3 about audience growth, maybe a short story serialized to your newsletter, and then segue all of your readers into a fallow period where you primarily will communicate with them via batch scheduled newsletters and social media posts before your next intense quarter six to twelve months later

A YEAR WITHOUT WRITING (MUCH)

And finally, here is an example of the full year mapped out for someone who has a nice big backlist of books, but only plans one new release in the next year.

This schedule assumes you have at least two series, each with more than three titles in it, and will be releasing two books, Series C, which is a Series 2.0 of Series A.

Each month will require work done in a previous month, so for example, in Month 0, the month before this year begins, you would be doing a flurry of work to prep for months 1-3, and then after that, each month would have a single task to prep for a few months out.

marketing: a year without writing (much) / WORKSHEET   ZOE YORK / ainsley booth

INSTRUCTIONS / months along the top, starting with next month; series/project groups down the side, sub-divide horizontally as needed

	Month 1	Month 2	Month 3	Month 4	Month 5	Month 6	Month 7	Month 8	Month 9	Month 10	Month 11	Month 12
SERIES A	Rebrand this series: new covers, new blurbs	FREE first in series campaign		CPC ad campaign on book #4	Books 1-3 boxed set release! 99 cents!		Book 4 FREE for a limited time					Cross promo with similar authors
SERIES B			Cross promo with similar authors							Rebrand this series: new covers, new blurbs	Free first in series campaign	
SERIES C						Newsletter push for new series		NEW RELEASE COMING! Social media blitz	BOOK 1 releases!!!!			

Month 1: re-brand backlist series A

Month 2: run a free first in series campaign on series A

Month 3: cross promo event for a book in series B

Month 4: CPC ad campaign for highest-concept book in series A

Month 5: release a box set for Series A, discount release price to 99 cents

Month 6: newsletter re-engagement campaign to begin pre-order push to new series C

Month 7: run a limited time free later-in-series book from series A

Month 8: ramp up to new series! Social media build!

Month 9: release book 1 in series C

Month 10: re-brand backlist series B

Month 11: run a free first in series campaign on series B

Month 12: cross promo event for a book in series A

Homework: Spend some time mocking up different schedules. Don't commit yourself to any of them until you've tried a few on for size—and then, once you launch yourself enthusiastically into a new plan, know that you can always start over again with a new month 0 planning period if a better idea comes to you.

CHAPTER NINETEEN

RELEASE SCHEDULES

HERE ARE my general thoughts on releasing a genre fiction series. This depends on if you are a debut author, a mid-list author, or an author with an eager and hungry fan base.

I'm going to assume that most people reading this book are either early in their careers, or have a good number of books under their belts but still want to take their brand and their series production to the next level.

If you are a debut author, with little to no platform, you want to get books one and two, and preferably the third as well, out in a reasonably quick time period. Some people advise all at once. I don't, and here's why: they might sink. And then what's your next step?

Books don't sink because they suck. (At least, not necessarily)

There are hundreds of thousands of contemporary romances available for sale on Amazon. Good books fade away every single day. Those aren't great odds, right? So I say play the conservative game and stagger your releases, so you can monitor how book one is doing, then how book one is doing, maybe do some packaging tweaking. Release book three while book four is in progress, etc.

My general rule is: Release a book when the next one is in production.

If you take six months to research a book before you start writing them, then you're going to want to sit on a finished book for a while before releasing it, IMO. You will hear counter opinions from other people, and they're not necessarily wrong. This is one of those decisions that has so many mitigating factors that the right answer is different for absolutely every person.

A LIST OF VARIOUS RELEASE SCHEDULES

- three books in the spring (Jan, March, May, or Feb, April, June); you write them, save them up, and release them in prime book buying season

- three releases equally staggered around the year (Jan, May, Sept)

Both of these schedules for your big series allow you time, probably, to write one or two smaller projects on the side, either release as a novella, or in a boxed set, or just get working ahead on future projects

- more aggressive, six to eight books in a year, every other month—this is gruelling, but it pays off for most people if the books are in one or two series and you're working the promo machine at the same time
- splitting books up to 10+ releases of serial parts and novellas (this is the same word count as above, most likely, and requires a bit more promo effort; genre dependent)
- less aggressive, one to two books a year, banking on your brand rising with each release; this works better in some genres than others (fantasy and new adult, maybe yes, cozies and contemporary romance, maybe only if you've got a horseshoe up your butt as

a debut, but definitely do-able with a bigger backlist to leverage for income)

What release schedules do you see working best in your genre? How do you feel about that? If you want to go a different way, what kinds of promo plans/questions do you have to try and make that work?

CHAPTER TWENTY

MARKETING A LOSS LEADER: STEP-BY-STEP HOW TO PUSH A FREE BOOK OR A 99 CENT DEAL

OVER AND OVER AGAIN IN this book, I have suggested that a free first-in-series is a great way to push a backlist series. Once you've done that, a later-in-series freebie also works. And 99 cent discounts can also work. All of these are loss leaders, like when a grocery store discounts butter to get you to shop there instead of at the competitors. They know they'll recoup the cost they're eating on the butter in the other groceries you buy.

You will maximize the sell-through from this freebie or 99 cent deal and earn more across the series if the books are meta-data connected and if the books clearly promise more of the same goodness—through tight series branding and hooks, continuing storylines, and protagonist teasing (a mysterious older brother? Definitely getting a book).

But what do I mean when I say, "spend a month pushing a first in series free"? What is the best schedule for a loss leader promotion?

You may hear people talk about "stacking ads" around a promo push. This usually means trying to get a Bookbub featured deal, then booking all the similar email blast deals (BargainBooksy/Freebooksy, Elite Reader, eReaderCafe, eReaderNewsToday, The Fussy Librarian, etc.) into the same week.

Generally, that week is the USA Today reporting period of Monday to Sunday, because if you're going to discount a book to 99 cents, it might be to try and hit a bestseller list by concentrating sales.

But what if you don't want to book a lot of ads?

Also, free books can't hit the bestseller list. So what if the book is free? Should you still stack?

There are a lot of different opinions out there. Here is mine: there's no value in stacking unless you're making a deliberate run for the bestseller lists, which is a reasonable thing to do in our business, but it's mostly an ego exercise. (I've done it many times … only two of my list-hits were truly a surprise, the others were all goals for that release/sale; so no judgement on that ego!)

TWO STRATEGIES FOR LOSS LEADER PROMOTION

A stacked, focused week

If you go this route for a 99 cent sale, you want to stack around a BookBub featured deal, and you want that deal to NOT be on a Sunday. I prefer a mid-week deal, but I'll take what I get.

Here is an example of a stacked promotion I did last year. I don't track all my promo like this, but I wanted to test all of these different sites because it had been ages since I'd used them.

	7	8	9	10	11	12	13	14	15	16
			M	T	W	Th	Fr	Sa	Sun	
			30-Sep	01-Oct	02-Oct	03-Oct	04-Oct	05-Oct	06-Oct	
			ManyBooks	Bargain Booksy	BookBub	Ainsley list	Romance ebook deals	Ereader Café	Fussy Librarian	
			Read Cheaply	Robin Reads		Zoe list	Happy Endings		Kindle Nation Daily	
				Booksends			Book Runes			
				Elite Reader						
				Ereader News Today						
			$64	$299	$955		$75	$25	$109	
LOVE IN A SANDSTORM PUSH RESULTS										
Kobo			16	12	71	53	17	11	7	
Amazon			266	468	1599	408	132	235	145	
D2D			44	62	413	158	23	43	34	
Google Play					35	18				
			326	542	2118	637	172	289	186	**4270**

But doubling up like that (or on some days, quadrupling up!) really makes it hard to assess which blasts are effective for your books and which are not.

Which is why, for free books, I much prefer to stretch out a promo for longer. And, I'd argue, if your goal is to move maximum units instead of hitting a list, it might be worthwhile to do the same with a 99 cent sale.

A full month

This does not need to be a calendar month, but that's good short hand, both for organization and for talking about the sale on social media.

Instead of the condensed schedule above, a full month might look like this (this is one I just made up; I don't track my free promo):

01-May	05-May	09-May	13-May	17-May	24-May	29-May	31-May
Zoe List	ManyBooks	Free Booksy	Booksends	Ereader News Today	BookBub	ereader café	Ainsley list

LOVE ON A SPRING MORNING PUSH RESULTS

CAN WE TALK ABOUT BOOKBUB?

I have mentioned this giant book marketing partner at least half a dozen times across this book, so it deserves its own sub-section of a chapter.

BookBub is not an ebook retailer (although they have branched into audiobook sales, via Chirp Books, and some industry observers think they may make a play for a corner of the ebook sales market in the future). Their primary business is a highly curated daily deal email, that authors and publishers pay to be featured in (the aforementioned Featured Deal).

These deals come with a reasonably high price tag, but due to the curated nature of their offerings, a reasonably good return on investment for the vast majority of titles listed.

In short, a BookBub Featured Deal is one of the most reliable marketing tools an author can use, *if* they can afford the upfront cost, and *if* they are able to secure a deal.

It's not accessible to all, especially writers living in poverty and who face economic barriers.

And while they accept a wide selection of books, across many genres, there are some authors who get rejected over and over again.

BookBub says they accept about 20% of the submissions they get most days, and their criteria is data-driven, so it can change frequently.

WHAT ARE THEY TRULY LOOKING FOR?

Books that might sell and/or drive sell through, because BookBub's business model is built on affiliate income.

So for free, they're looking for first in a series in a genre that has historically done well for them. They want books that are well edited, well reviewed, with a professional cover*, <u>that will meet the expectations of the subscribers in that genre.</u> This last point makes it hard to get a BookBub if what you write doesn't fall squarely in the centre of a genre that they promote. If you write sweet contemporary romance, for example, that's a bit harder of a sell than a sexy contemp. (Try Women's Fiction!) If you write sci-fi romance, that's hard, because they don't have a list for that—you can sometimes get an ad in paranormal romance, but that's not quite the right audience. Etc.

WHAT SETS BOOKBUB APART FROM ALL OTHER READER-DEAL LISTS?

- They curate their deal offerings more than most other sites
- They aggressively build their list, targeting people who don't know they can get cheap books on their phone or tablet

The combination of these two factors means they have a good list of hungry-for-ebook readers, and good quality offerings for those readers, who trust the reputation of BookBub, and continue to open their emails and click on offers.

WHAT'S THE BEST WAY TO GET THE BANG OUT OF THE BOOKBUB BUCK?

- it is absolutely critical that your deal book be metadata connected to other books in a series. Do a website and retailer double check—do you have all the books linked in the way you want readers to read-through the series?
- maximize the length of your series. If you're doing a deal on #1, and you've got #2 and #3 out, and #4 is in the works, get a pre-order up.
- pay attention to what your social media pages are doing during BookBub week—you want them book focused!
- Do you have a reader group? Put a link to it in the back of your book. And in general, max out the back matter of that book.
- This one is more advanced: Put a pixel on your website, and in the weeks after BookBub, do a targeted Facebook ad to visitors about the series they just got the freebie for.

CHAPTER TWENTY-ONE

10 FIVE-MINUTE MARKETING HACKS

HERE ARE some bonus lists for when you want to get your marketing act together but frankly, it's all a bit hard. Set a timer for five minutes, and do ONE thing.

———

10 FIVE-MINUTE MARKETING HACKS

1. Read one of your books! Highlight a few lines you love and share a screen shot or photo of them on social media. *Don't forget buy links.*

2. Make a header image for social media and your news-

letter that features a series. A photo of the paperbacks stacked or all the ebook covers lined up works well. *Don't forget your author name and the series name ... and buy links.*

3. Apply for a BookBub featured deal on a free first in series. *The book can already be free, or you can wait until they accept it to make it free.*

4. Make a new media kit for your bestselling book. *Go back and grab those favourite lines you shared the other day and include those as new excerpts!*

5. Write a conversation between two favourite characters. Send it out in your next newsletter. *Don't forget buy links.*

6. Invite another author to do the same, and post those conversations on your blog or social media. Link to each other! *Don't forget buy links.*

7. Pick a backlist book (not free) that is connected to your next release, and set it up as a free download link on BookFunnel or directly off your website.

8. Go live in your private Facebook group. Just to say hi!

Don't worry if nobody sees it, or few people respond. Here's a script: "I'm trying to step out of my comfort zone, and I've heard Facebook really likes live videos, so let's give this a try. This week, I'm trying to write [Book title], which is connected to [Book that's already out]. If you haven't read that one, let me know in the comments and I'll share a copy with you!"

9. Spend five minutes watching Instagram posts or stories or Facebook stories. Skip any that don't interest you. This is research! Research is work, too! Make notes of any ideas you see that you might like to try.

10. Write a five point list of evergreen content that could be posted from time to time on social media: meet a character, series lists, trope match game, this or that, perennial reader questions.

CHAPTER TWENTY-TWO

RE-BRANDING YOURSELF: STARTING OVER COMPLETELY

MAYBE I SHOULDN'T BURY this chapter right at the end, but it didn't slide in neatly anywhere else. It's not even a full chapter, to be honest. It's a simple acknowledgement that this, too, is an option in a marketing plan.

One form of radical self-care is giving yourself a do-over, on your own terms. And sometimes, a new pen name is a sound business decision as well. When those two conditions are met at the same time, starting over completely can be an excellent plan.

I like a new pen name for a new words more than partitioning off backlist books under a new name (although that has its place in some plans). I don't think a new name is required for a new genre, but it is always nice to be a debut author. When I wrote Hate F*@k, there was a certain boost from it being "Ainsley Booth's erotic romance debut", which is not a lie. If I were to write a cozy mystery, for example, I might write it under another name. Or I might not! That's the thing about plans, they shift a lot depending on what else is going on.

There is also baggage that can accumulate around a pen name: sales slumps, abandoned series, genre hopping. All of that is life, which just happens. But it can bog us down when we're thinking about reinventing our brand with a shiny new plan.

For some people, the shiny new plan is best implemented on a shiny new name.

If reading that sentence just gave you a strange sense of lightness, and maybe you want permission to just do it—do it. And don't look back. I'm excited for you!

CHAPTER TWENTY-THREE

CONCLUSION

AS YOU CLOSE THIS BOOK, and pick up your pen, remember that we aren't publishing by committee here. The best plan for you is the one that feels right, tracks with your principles, and will point you in the direction of your long term goals.

When I say, the best marketing you can do is write the next book, I don't mean write it faster. I mean, if you keep writing what you want to write deep down, that story that feeds a fire in your belly? You will get there faster than if you follow someone else's paint by numbers plan.

Even mine.

My hope for you is that right now, you have a plan

for a new series. You understand your backlist better, and have a plan to manage that in an on-going way.

Maybe you have a new five-year plan focused on what you want to have written down the road...and what course-corrections need to happen now to get on the right path.

But if you don't yet, if you're still processing all of this, *that is okay, too.*

You might need to muddle through a few more titles before you hit upon clarity and the plan clicks into place. Some of us have to write ten books to figure out what we really want to write in our *next* ten books.

(For me, it was six books for one pen name, and three for the other, which is really...nine is almost ten!)

In 2014, I read a post by Courtney Milan on a web forum called Kboards about Regions of Discoverability, and the struggle I had been experiencing was suddenly very clear. I felt seen in a way I hadn't before in online discussions about publishing.

It's not fair—but nothing in business is—that it takes some people longer to be "discovered" by readers than others. And yet most of what we hear out there is that if we are not being discovered at a Good Hustle Rate, it's because we're doing something wrong.

First of all, wrong is an unnecessarily loaded term there.

Second of all, you can do everything "right" and it just won't click for random, who-knows reasons.

This book is my contribution to that conversation, an attempt to provide balance and a bit of hope— because I believe those Regions of Discoverability are navigable for everyone. To move through them, though, we need to understand what they are and what we are doing, objectively, and then decide if now is the right time to put the time and/or money into the effort to jump to the next level. It might not be. There is nothing wrong opting out of the Hustle Race, and Ms. Milan remains a great example of this approach to publishing six years later.

But at certain points in our careers, when we are full of enthusiasm, it's so much easier to make those advances when we understand the context around a marketing plan, and why some just work and other plans flounder.

If you ever want to chat about *your* plan, I'm pretty available on Twitter and YouTube, @zoeyorkwrites in both places, and you can subscribe to my monthly writing newsletter at www.romanceyourbrand.com.

ALSO BY ZOE YORK

If you like small town romances... **try my Wardham series**

Between Then and Now

What Once Was Perfect

Where Their Hearts Collide

When They Weren't Looking

Beyond Love and Hate

No Time Like Forever

Perfect No Matter What

Beneath These Bright Stars

Forever Begins with a Kiss

All That They Desire

If you like Navy SEALs ... **SEALs Undone**

Fall Out

Fall Hard

Fall Away

Fall Deep

Fall Fast

Fall Back

Fall Dark

Fall Dirty

Fall Quiet

Fall Easy

If you like military heroes in a small town setting... **Pine Harbour**

Love in a Small Town

Love in a Snowstorm

Love on a Spring Morning

Love on a Summer Night

Love on the Run

Love in a Sandstorm

Love on the Outskirts of Town

Love on the Edge of Reason

And finally ... **Vikings in Space!**

A Viking's Peace

A Viking's Bride

A Viking's Need

For a complete list of my books after this book is published, please visit my website:

www.zoeyork.com

If you like silly, sexy, over the top fairy tale romances…
Billionaire Secrets

Undercover Billionaire
Her Billionaire Best Friend
A Billionaire for Christmas

Want to know more?
www.ainsleybooth.com

CPSIA information can be obtained
at www.ICGtesting.com
Printed in the USA
LVHW091507060222
710388LV00006B/977